THE VIETNAM WAR

CHRONICLE OF AMERICA'S WARS

Debbie Levy

LERNER PUBLICATIONS COMPANY

MINNEAPOLIS

Lerner Publications Company
A division of Lerner Publishing Group
241 First Avenue North
Minneapolis, MN 55401

Website address: www.lernerbooks.com

Library of Congress Cataloging-in-Publication Data

Levy, Debbie.
    The Vietnam War / by Debbie Levy.
        p.   cm. — (Chronicle of America's wars)
    Includes bibliographical references and index.
    ISBN: 0–8225–0421–9 (lib. bdg. : alk. paper)
    1. Vietnamese Conflict, 1961–1975—United States—Juvenile literature. 2. United States—History—1961–1969—Juvenile literature. 3. United States—History—1969—Juvenile literature. [1. Vietnamese Conflict, 1961–1975. 2. Vietnam—History.] I. Title. II. Series.
DS558.L475 2004
959.704'3—dc21   2002156558

Manufactured in the United States of America
1 2 3 4 5 6 – JR – 09 08 07 06 05 04

TABLE OF CONTENTS

INTRODUCTION

The speaker climbed the steps and faced the crowd gathered in the square. People pressed against each other to hear what the frail, bearded man had to say.

"All men are created equal," he began. "They are endowed by their Creator with certain unalienable rights, among these are Life, Liberty, and the pursuit of Happiness."

The speaker looked at the crowd. Then he asked: "Do you hear me distinctly, my fellow countrymen?"

The crowd was silent for a moment. But their answer was not delayed for long.

"Yes, we hear you!"

The speaker at this gathering was not Thomas Jefferson, although he spoke Jefferson's words. The year was not 1776, when Jefferson penned these words in the Declaration of Independence. The speaker was Ho Chi Minh, and the date was September 2, 1945. He spoke in the city of Hanoi, in the country of Vietnam. And he was declaring Vietnam's independence from France, which had controlled Vietnam since the mid-1800s.

Ho Chi Minh had obtained a copy of the U.S. Declaration of Independence from Americans who were in Southeast Asia in the closing days of World War II (1939–1945). Ho, as he was called, led a group called the Viet Minh. The Viet Minh and the Americans had worked together

during World War II against Japan, America's wartime enemy in Asia.

After the surrender of Japan on August 15, 1945, the Viet Minh had taken control of the northern part of Vietnam. Ho formed a government, and he hoped for support from the United States. After all, the Americans had just fought a world war to preserve individual freedoms and national independence.

But history took a different turn. Instead of supporting Ho Chi Minh, Americans came to view him and the Viet Minh as a threat. For although Ho's goal was independence, he was also a Communist. The United States viewed the economic and political system of Communism as a threat to the U.S. systems of democracy and capitalism. Opposed to Communism, the United States opposed the Viet Minh in their war against the French. When the Viet Minh successfully drove the French out of Vietnam in the 1950s, the Americans moved in to try to stop the Viet Minh from spreading Communism throughout Vietnam. Slowly but surely, the world's most powerful nation went to war—and, for the first time in its history, it lost.

1 A HISTORY OF STRUGGLE

Vietnam is a long strip of land on the eastern part of the Indochinese Peninsula in Southeast Asia. Its shoreline faces the South China Sea and Pacific Ocean to the east. It shares a northern border with China. To the west are Laos and Cambodia. With 1,000 miles of coastline and 128,000 square miles of land, Vietnam is about the size and shape of a slimmed-down California.

All of Vietnam lies in the tropics, close to the equator, where the weather is warm year-round. But the north and south differ in climate and terrain. In the north, hills and mountains rise over large plains and river basins. These include the Red River basin, a heavily populated farming area. Violent monsoons (seasonal winds) bring rain and often cause rivers to flood, destroying crops and livestock.

In southern Vietnam, the Mekong River dominates the landscape. The waterway splits into smaller waterways as it approaches the South China Sea. This area of small rivers, the Mekong River Delta, benefits from rich soil. It is the country's leading producer of rice.

Central Vietnam is a narrow belt that connects north and south. Mountains form the western border. Farmers grow crops such as rubber trees, tea plants, and coffee on the region's plateaus.

Vietnam's shoreline harbors beautiful beaches. Valuable minerals such as coal, iron, and bauxite lie beneath the country's soil. And, as those who came to conquer the nation discovered, Vietnam is a land of dense jungles—perfect places from which to launch surprise attacks on foreign enemies.

OCCUPIED TERRITORY

Invasion by outsiders has been a part of Vietnam's legacy since its early history. As early as 208 B.C., Chinese forces moved south to take over northern Vietnam. For one thousand years, China ruled this region.

The Vietnamese people constantly fought their conquerors. In the tenth century A.D., the Chinese emperor agreed to allow Vietnam to be an independent state. But fighting resumed when later Chinese rulers invaded again. It was not until 1426 that Vietnam became fully independent of Chinese rule.

Still, Vietnam was not peaceful. The region was torn by civil wars, as different families bid to lead the nation. Into this unstable environment came a new power—Europeans.

MERCHANTS AND MISSIONARIES

In the 1600s, merchants from Portugal, England, France, and Holland established trading posts in southern Vietnam, which the Europeans called Cochinchina. Along with the merchants came Roman Catholic missionaries, or religious teachers. Most of these people were French, and their mission was to convert Vietnamese people to the Roman Catholic faith. Hundreds of thousands of Vietnamese converted from Buddhism, the traditional religion of Vietnam, to Catholicism in the 1600s. By the late 1600s, conflicts between northern and southern Vietnamese discouraged many European traders from doing business in Vietnam.

In the late 1700s, French businessmen provided soldiers and supplies to help Nguyen Anh, head of one of the families competing for power in Vietnam, take over the country. In exchange, France received trading rights and territory. At the city of Hue in central Vietnam, Nguyen Anh renamed himself Emperor Gia Long.

Despite the French role in creating the Nguyen dynasty (family of rulers), Gia Long's successors were suspicious of foreign missionaries and merchants. Vietnamese emperors of the 1800s harassed the foreigners and even tortured Catholics.

In response to the inhumane treatment of Catholics and to protect French business interests, France sent ships and soldiers to Vietnam. To ensure peace, Emperor Tu Duc gave France control of the territory around Saigon, which lies in southern Vietnam, in 1862. Although many people in France opposed colonialism (the conquest and control of foreign territories), others were eager to extend French power. By 1883 the French had conquered all of Vietnam as well as neighboring Laos and Cambodia. This region came to be called French Indochina.

DID YOU KNOW?
Around the time the French conquered Saigon in 1862, Tu Duc sent a letter to U.S. president Abraham Lincoln seeking American assistance. Lincoln did not reply.

FAST FACT

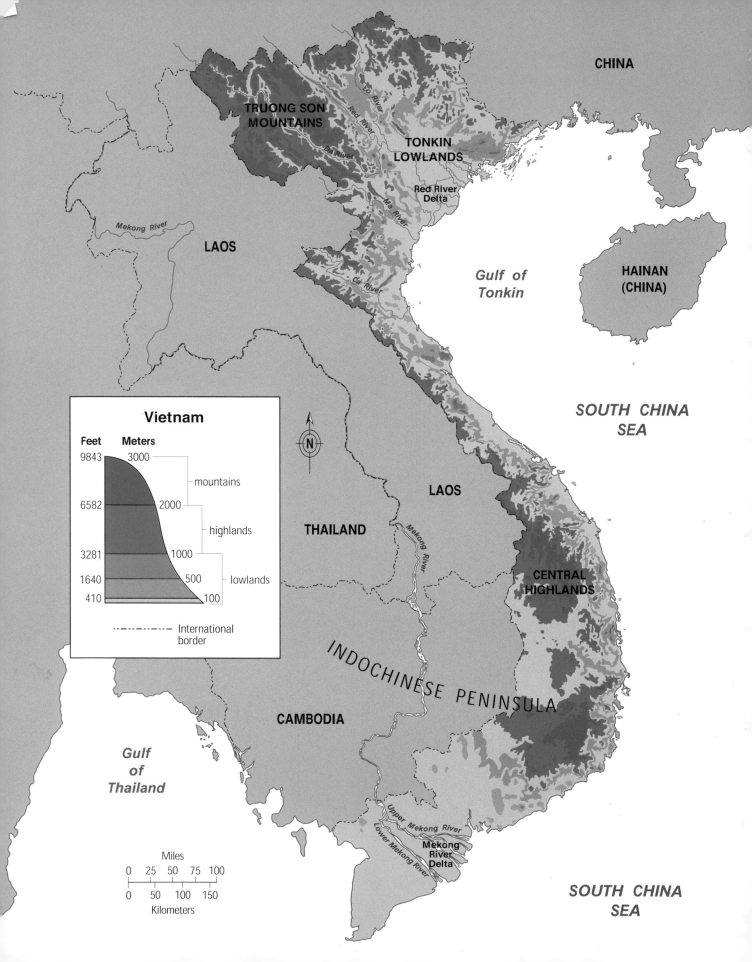

CHINA

TRUONG SON
MOUNTAINS

Lo River

Red River

TONKIN
LOWLANDS

Da River

Red River
Delta

Ma River

Mekong River

LAOS

Ca River

**Gulf of
Tonkin**

HAINAN
(CHINA)

**SOUTH CHINA
SEA**

Vietnam

Feet	Meters	
9843	3000	mountains
6582	2000	highlands
3281	1000	
1640	500	lowlands
410	100	

-··-··- International
border

N

LAOS

THAILAND

CENTRAL
HIGHLANDS

INDOCHINESE PENINSULA

CAMBODIA

**Gulf
of
Thailand**

Upper Mekong River

Lower Mekong River

Mekong
River
Delta

**SOUTH CHINA
SEA**

Miles

0   25 50 75 100

0   50 100 150

Kilometers

LIFE UNDER FRENCH COLONIALISM

For some Vietnamese, life under French rule was very good. Local people who served in the colonial government enjoyed comfortable lives. The children of these officials often received a good education at private schools. Many studied at universities in Paris, the capital of France.

Most Vietnamese, however, did not enjoy the good life. Many farmers had been forced to abandon their land during the French invasion. These vacated farms were given to French colonial settlers. Thus, many Vietnamese peasants (poor farmers) found themselves with no land to farm. To survive, these peasants worked in mines and on plantations, large farms owned by French colonists. They raised rice, produced rubber, and mined coal, often under miserable conditions and for little pay. By World War II,

France was earning a great deal of money from the sale of goods produced in Vietnam.

But Vietnam's productivity did not benefit most Vietnamese. Some citizens organized to resist French rule. They viewed themselves as nationalists, fighting for the right to govern themselves. These people produced publications that argued for independence. They also organized labor strikes and staged violent uprisings against French rule. The French crushed the uprisings and imprisoned many nationalist leaders. Many more nationalist leaders fled the country. These actions imposed order in the restless colony. But it was a shaky order.

"NGUYEN THE PATRIOT"

Ho Chi Minh became the most influential nationalist leader in Vietnam. He had been born Nguyen Sinh Cung in 1890 in central

Hanoi under French rule. French rule was designed to benefit French colonizers and a small percentage of Vietnamese who worked with them. Most Vietnamese citizens received low wages and paid high taxes.

Vietnam. As a young man, Ho had left Vietnam and traveled all over the world. By 1920 he was living in Paris, where he took the name Nguyen Ai Quoc—"Nguyen the Patriot." Communism had recently been established in the Soviet Union, a large union of states that was dominated by Russia, and Nguyen joined the new Communist Party in France. Under Soviet Communism, the central Communist Party controlled the economy, as well as the government and the military. Most private property was outlawed. The Communist Party was in charge of distributing goods and services. People were supposed to work and contribute to society according to their abilities. In return, they would share in society's goods according to their needs. In reality, Communism did not work this fairly. Still, supporters of Communism believed that this system would improve life for ordinary citizens. Communists also stood for anticolonialism—exactly what Nguyen wanted to hear.

From 1920 on, Nguyen Ai Quoc worked to create a Communist revolution in Vietnam. He attended a school in the Soviet Union for Asian revolutionaries. In 1930, while living in Hong Kong, China, he helped found the Indochinese Communist Party. This group called for an independent Vietnam.

World War II broke out in 1939, as Nazi Germany set out to conquer Europe. At the same time, Japan sought to rule all of Asia. By 1940 the Nazis had overrun France. They set up a government in the south called Vichy France, run by pro-Nazi French officials. That same year, Japan took over Vietnam, but the Japanese allowed a pro-Vichy French government to continue

Ho Chi Minh in 1930. A friend described Ho as having "only one thought in his head, his country, Vietnam."

to run the country. In 1941 the Japanese attacked the U.S. naval base at Pearl Harbor in the Hawaiian Islands, bringing the United States into the fight against Japan and Germany.

BIRTH OF THE VIET MINH

That same year, disguised as a Chinese journalist, Nguyen Ai Quoc returned to Vietnam for the first time in thirty years. Together with other Vietnamese revolutionaries, including Pham Van Dong and Vo Nguyen Giap, Nguyen Ai Quoc formed the Viet Minh, or Vietnam Independence League. At this time, "Nguyen the Patriot" took the name Ho Chi Minh—meaning "Bringer of Light" or "Enlightened Leader."

Viet Minh membership was open to Communists, as well as to non-Communist Vietnamese who shared the goal of fighting foreign rule. But the group's leadership was Communist. Although the United States opposed Communism, it was willing to work with the Viet Minh Communists against their common World War II enemy, Japan. (Similarly, the United States and the Communist Soviet Union were allies in World War II against Nazi Germany.)

Ho Chi Minh and his followers helped the United States by striking Japanese forces in the Vietnamese jungles and by rescuing American pilots shot down by the Japanese. For a brief period toward the end of World War II, American soldiers even trained Viet Minh soldiers. According to historian Stanley Karnow, Ho told a U.S. official that he would welcome "a million American soldiers . . . but no French." Ho's military leader, General Vo Nguyen Giap, regarded the United States as a "good friend" because "it is a democracy without territorial ambitions."

In early August 1945, the United States dropped two atomic bombs on Japan, destroying two major cities and killing thousands of civilians. On August 15, 1945, Japan surrendered. (Nazi Germany had already surrendered in May.) The day after Japan's surrender, Ho Chi Minh and other Vietnamese leaders formed a new, independent Vietnamese government, called the Democratic Republic of Vietnam, with Ho as president. The new government was seated in Hanoi in northern Vietnam. Its members were mostly Communists, but the government also included Catholics and other groups. Throughout the country, Communist forces attempted to seize control of local governments. These efforts were successful in the north, where the Viet Minh took control of Hanoi. Communist forces did not have as much support in the south, however. They managed to take control of Saigon on August 25.

On September 2, 1945, Ho Chi Minh stood before half a million people in Hanoi and read the Vietnamese declaration of

American bombers dropped atomic bombs on the Japanese cities of Nagasaki (below) and Hiroshima in August 1945. Japan quickly surrendered, and Ho Chi Minh declared Vietnam's independence.

independence. He started with the famous American words, "All men are created equal." That same day, Japan signed formal surrender documents, officially ending World War II in the Pacific. But for Vietnam, the war was only beginning.

CHAOS IN VIETNAM

Despite the declarations of Ho Chi Minh, Vietnam's independence was far from certain. France—once again ruled by its prewar leaders—had no intention of giving up its colony. These leaders reasserted France's claim to its colony. Some U. S. officials opposed this claim. But U.S. president Harry S. Truman did not want to disagree with France, one of its most important European allies. So the United States did not interfere with the restoration of French rule in Vietnam.

President Harry S. Truman

Violence convulsed Vietnam. In the south, French soldiers battled with Viet Minh fighters. By October French forces once again controlled Saigon. In the north, some Viet Minh groups went on murderous rampages. They killed many Vietnamese whom they considered loyal to the colonialist system.

By October 1945, approximately 35,000 French soldiers and government officials were in Vietnam. They established a new government in Saigon, giving positions of authority to pro-French Vietnamese. Ho Chi Minh decided to negotiate. France and the Democratic Republic of Vietnam reached a compromise in March 1946: The Viet Minh would not resist the return of a small number of French troops to northern Vietnam. In turn, France would allow Ho's government to remain independent.

Ho traveled to Paris for further talks. While he was there, however, in June 1946, the French high commissioner in Vietnam declared a separate French-controlled "Republic of Cochinchina" in south Vietnam. This action trampled the March agreement. In December Viet Minh forces attacked French bases in Hanoi. Soon the French and Viet Minh were at war.

THE FIRST VIETNAM WAR

With superior weapons, French troops quickly chased Ho Chi Minh and his poorly armed Viet Minh fighters out of Hanoi. By November 1946, the French occupied the northern capital and seemed certain of swift victory throughout Vietnam.

But the Viet Minh's guerrilla tactics— attacking in small groups and then slipping away—were effective against the French.

French artillery firing on a Viet Minh position. The United States provided the French with billions of dollars in financial support during the war.

The Viet Minh also worked successfully to win over the Vietnamese people. They offered land, health care, and educational programs to pro-Viet Minh villages. And the Viet Minh dealt violently with people who favored the French.

By December 1946, the Viet Minh army had recruited enough fighters to launch its first big assault on the French. "The resistance will be long and arduous [difficult]," said commanding General Vo Nguyen Giap, "but our cause is just and we will surely triumph."

Former Vietnamese emperor Bao Dai became head of the French-controlled government. France established a local Vietnamese army in the south. While the French and its Vietnamese allies controlled most of Vietnam's cities, the Communist Viet Minh controlled much of the countryside in the northern part of the country.

AMERICA'S PROBLEM

At first, the United States did not take sides in the war. But by the 1950s, global events prompted the United States to back France—and to become even more anti-Viet Minh than the French.

The spread of Communism pushed the United States in this direction. After World War II, the Soviet Union installed Communist governments in many Eastern European countries. The People's Republic of China—Vietnam's neighbor and the world's most populous nation—also had a Communist government.

In January 1950, China and the Soviet Union formally recognized Ho Chi Minh's regime, or rule, as the rightful government of Vietnam. These countries began supplying weapons, trucks, and military advisers to the Viet Minh.

Alarmed by these events, President Harry Truman officially recognized the French-supported Bao Dai government in February 1950. Not all U.S. officials agreed with this move. One wrote, "Whether the French like it or not, independence is coming to Indochina. Why, therefore, do we tie ourselves to the tail of their battered kite?"

Despite these warnings, American leaders framed the conflict in Vietnam as a global battle between Communism and democracy. Yet the French colonial government in Vietnam was not really a democracy. It did not represent the Vietnamese people. President Truman and his successor, President Dwight Eisenhower, understood this situation. But to U.S. leaders at the time, nearly any regime was better than a Communist government.

Containment—containing, or limiting, Communism—became the guiding light in U.S. foreign policy.

In June 1950, this containment policy faced its biggest test. On June 25, 1950, Communist North Korea invaded democratic South Korea. The North Koreans received military assistance and encouragement from China and the Soviet Union. For many Americans, this attack proved that Communists would not hesitate to conquer neighboring countries. The United States, joined by many of its allies in the United Nations (an international organization created after World War II to preserve peace), sent troops to drive back the North Koreans. The war was difficult and bloody, costing nearly 37,000 American lives in three years. In July 1953,

U.S. soldiers during the Korean War. The American policy of containing Communism would face its biggest challenges in Asia.

French paratroopers protect the landing of their fellow soldiers at Dien Bien Phu in 1953.

the Korean War ended with the withdrawal of North Korean troops from South Korea.

Influenced by the Korean conflict, the United States stepped up its aid to the French in Vietnam. By the mid-1950s, the United States was paying 80 percent of France's expenses for the war in Vietnam. A small number of U.S. military advisers also went to Vietnam to help the French.

THE DEFEAT OF THE FRENCH

In November 1953, French soldiers overtook the village of Dien Bien Phu, on the northwest border of Vietnam. They built a fort of bunkers and outpost buildings protected by troops.

Viet Minh General Giap had an ambitious plan. He wanted to surround Dien Bien Phu and trap the French. To make such a strategy effective, he needed to move heavy weapons up into the mountains towering over the valley where the French had dug in. This movement had to be accomplished secretly so the Viet Minh could mount a surprise attack. The task seemed impossible, given the rugged terrain and the size and weight of the weapons.

Viet Minh soldiers and civilians (non-soldiers) dragged huge pieces of artillery—called Iron Elephants—by hand up the mountains. There they hid the guns in the mouths of caves.

In March 1954, the Viet Minh began their assault. The French were taken by surprise and outnumbered. After Viet Minh shelling ruined the Dien Bien Phu airstrip, the French could not fly in or out of their fort. All they could do was wait for help, or for death.

The Viet Minh kept the French under siege at Dien Bien Phu throughout April 1954. As the trapped French troops ran out of supplies and water, the Viet Minh hacked tunnels and trenches in the earth, inching toward the walls of the fort.

France turned to the United States for help. President Eisenhower was distressed about the possibility of a Communist Vietnam. If Vietnam became a Communist nation, he said, the remaining countries in Southeast Asia would "go over very quickly" to Communism, like a "row of dominoes." He added: "The possible consequences of the loss are just incalculable to the free world."

Despite his concerns, President Eisenhower did not come to the rescue of the French. This was partly because important members of the U.S. Congress were opposed to U.S. involvement. The surviving French soldiers at Dien Bien Phu surrendered to the Viet Minh on May 7, 1954. Unable to defeat the Viet Minh, the French decided to negotiate an end to the war.

The war between France and the Viet Minh had lasted eight years. Even with billions of dollars of U.S. aid and superior weapons, the French had lost. The U.S. policy of containment in Asia was in trouble. The Communist-led Viet Minh prepared to govern the northern region of Vietnam again. Would the United States let this Communist "domino" fall?

The Viet Minh leaders knew the United States would continue to oppose Communism. "When we received news of the Dien Bien Phu victory, everyone practically jumped into the air, they were so happy about it," said General Vo Nguyen Giap in an interview forty-two years later. "But Ho Chi Minh said that this is only . . . the first step: we have yet to fight the Americans. It was very clear then."

French soldiers at Dien Bien Phu. The French had badly underestimated the Viet Minh's ability to surround and attack the fort.

DEADLY
2 DOMINOES

After the French defeat at Dien Bien Phu, representatives from several nations met in Geneva, Switzerland, to discuss the situation. Called the Geneva Conference on Indochina, the meeting included representatives from the United States, Great Britain, France, the Soviet Union, Laos, Cambodia, and both competing governments in Vietnam—Bao Dai's pro-French regime and the Viet Minh. On July 20, 1954, the nations signed a document called the Geneva Agreement, which granted independence to Vietnam, Laos, and Cambodia—all former French colonies. The agreement also temporarily divided Vietnam, giving power to the Viet Minh in the north and to Bao Dai's government in the south. The agreement provided for a nationwide

vote within two years to choose a government for a unified Vietnam.

French soldiers left the country. Nine hundred thousand Vietnamese in the north, mostly Catholics, moved to South Vietnam. Catholic Vietnamese felt more welcomed by the non-Communist regime, because many Communists consider religious worship a threat to the Communist system. One hundred thousand pro-Communist southerners moved to North Vietnam. Quietly, thousands of Viet Minh supporters remained in the south, poised to harass the government there.

THE SOUTH'S NEW LEADER

In the south, Bao Dai named Ngo Dinh Diem prime minister. Diem was Catholic,

Ngo Dinh Diem

and like many of the Catholics in Vietnam and elsewhere, he was strongly opposed to Communism. For this stance, he gained the strong support of the United States.

Diem quickly overshadowed Bao Dai. In October 1955, he became president of the newly proclaimed Republic of South Vietnam. Diem named his relatives to high-level government jobs. His armed forces dealt brutally with opponents. Diem favored Catholics, giving them land taken from Buddhist landowners. Diem also angered many peasants by failing to change the system of land ownership in Vietnam that favored wealthy landowners.

The United States supported Diem with economic and military assistance and advisers. The U.S. government also urged him to make his government more democratic. But Diem did not do so.

TURMOIL IN THE NORTH

Back in power in North Vietnam, Ho Chi Minh's government faced the ravages left by the war against France. Factories, railroads, roads, and bridges were in ruins. The Soviets helped North Vietnam buy emergency supplies of rice to feed the North Vietnamese population. China provided weapons and political advisers to help the North Vietnamese Communists establish firm control. Ho Chi Minh created a disastrous program that was supposed to give land back to peasants. In the process, tens of thousands of people were imprisoned or executed because they supposedly owned too much land,

The brutal war with the French left much of Vietnam in ruins. The world's two major Communist powers, China and the Soviet Union, helped the North Vietnamese.

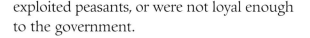

exploited peasants, or were not loyal enough to the government.

STEPS TO WAR

The July 1956 Geneva Agreement deadline for elections for the leadership of the entire country came and went without a vote. President Diem insisted that the Communist regime in the north could not be trusted to run a fair election. The country would remain divided.

In May 1957, Diem met with President Eisenhower in Washington, D.C. The U.S. president called Diem the "miracle man" of Asia. "The cost of defending freedom, of defending America, must be paid in many forms and in many places . . . [and] military as well as economic help is currently needed in Vietnam," Eisenhower said.

However, Diem's focus in Vietnam was control, not freedom. His government was

President Dwight D. Eisenhower provided economic aid to the South Vietnamese government.

so preoccupied with putting down criticism of his rule that it did little to address citizens' needs, such as medical care and education. The Viet Minh promised a better life—although their record in the north, especially with brutal land reform, was not encouraging.

A wide range of South Vietnamese—peasants, professionals, youth leaders, artists, and others—organized the National Liberation Front (NLF) of South Vietnam in 1958. The NLF called for the overthrow of Diem, and end to the American presence in Vietnam, and the reunification of Vietnam. In areas in the south where the NLF gained support, it ran the government and provided services to the people.

Diem and his U.S. allies believed the NLF was only a mouthpiece of the North Vietnamese Communists, who were known in the south as Viet Cong, for Vietnamese Communists. In fact, the Communist Party did help form the NLF. But the NLF also included non-Communists who viewed Diem as a dictator and who wanted an end to foreign interference in Vietnam. Some NLF members worked for the Diem government while secretly supporting the NLF.

The Viet Cong also gained more influence and control in South Vietnam through violence and terror. They bombed buildings and assassinated thousands of people loyal to the Diem government. The leaders of North Vietnam created a special Central Office of South Vietnam to run the war in the south. They sent guerrillas south along the roads and pathways of the Ho Chi Minh Trail—a route along South Vietnam's western border passing through parts of southern Laos and Cambodia.

"WE SHALL PAY ANY PRICE"

In January 1961, Soviet premier Nikita Khrushchev gave a speech in which he said the Soviet Union would "wholeheartedly" support wars of "national liberation"—such as "the armed struggle waged by the people of Vietnam." Fears of Communist threats like this one caused U.S. policymakers to stick by their anti-Communist ally, even though they were disturbed by his violent actions against his own people.

John F. Kennedy became the new U.S. president on January 20, 1961. The threat of Communism was very much on his mind. Just as Krushchev pledged to support armed struggles around the world, the new American president pledged to protect liberty. "Let every nation know," he said in his inaugural address, "whether it wishes us well or ill, that we shall pay any price, bear any burden, meet any hardship, support any friend, oppose any foe to assure the survival and the success of liberty."

In 1961 the Viet Cong increased its attacks on President Diem's regime. Diem asked the new U.S. president for additional military aid. President Kennedy sent several hundred Green Berets—the U.S. Army's highly trained Special Forces soldiers—to serve as military advisers. These men trained South Vietnamese soldiers in anti-guerrilla warfare.

President Kennedy soon sent additional military advisers to Vietnam. Then came U.S. helicopters, with pilots and crews. These helicopters, flown by Americans, carried South Vietnamese troops into fighting zones. Americans were in combat situations, even if they were not technically combat soldiers.

Soon Americans began to die in combat. James Thomas Davis, a twenty-five-year-old army specialist, was the first American combat death. He was killed by Viet Cong gunfire near Saigon on December 22, 1961. In a letter to his father, Davis had written, "I don't feel too badly about having to be here when I think of all the potential good it will have for this country."

ANGRY CITIZENS

In 1962 President Diem created a new program that forced people in the countryside

Military Advisers

Before there were American troops in Vietnam, there were "military advisers." These were generally members of the U.S. armed forces, but they were not in Vietnam to fight. Their job was to train South Vietnamese soldiers and to help South Vietnamese military leaders plan strategy. On the other side, China and the Soviet Union sent their own military advisers to assist North Vietnam.

to leave their farms and live in special villages surrounded by trenches and guarded by soldiers. The villages, called strategic hamlets, were meant to shield the peasants from the Viet Cong. Most peasants were not happy about the forced resettlement. The strategic hamlet program turned some peasants into Viet Cong supporters—not the result Diem desired.

Angry peasants were not Diem's only problem. Many Buddhists also opposed the Catholic president. Diem's government forbade the flying of Buddhist flags, even at temples. In May 1963, Buddhists protested this ban in the ancient city of Hue. South Vietnamese police fired on the crowd of demonstrators, killing eleven of them.

Then, on June 11, 1963, the Buddhists staged a dramatic protest that captured the attention of the entire world. Quang Duc, a seventy-three-year-old Buddhist monk, made his way to a busy street in Saigon. Following close behind were 250 other monks, as well as Buddhist nuns. At Le Van Duyet Street, Quang Duc sat down in the street. He closed his eyes. Another monk poured a gasoline mixture on him and stepped away. Quang Duc calmly struck a match. Fire engulfed him, burning him to death.

Photographs of this suicide by fire were printed in newspapers everywhere. More Buddhist protest suicides followed. President Diem asked his brother, Ngo Dinh Nhu, to deal with the situation. Nhu raided Buddhist pagodas, or temples, and arrested monks and nuns. Nhu's wife, Madame Ngo Dinh Nhu, commented

Quang Duc brought worldwide attention to the unfair treatment of Vietnamese Buddhists by burning himself to death on June 11, 1963. The act sparked condemnation of Ngo Dinh Diem's regime.

coldly: "All the Buddhists have done for this country is to barbecue a monk."

DIEM'S DOWNFALL

Diem's U.S. supporters were horrified by these events. Privately, U.S. policymakers doubted whether Diem could continue to lead his country. Publicly, they said that Diem needed to reform his government. High-ranking South Vietnamese military officers began talking about a coup, or overthrow, against Diem. Some U.S. officials encouraged the plotters. President Kennedy did not discourage them.

On November 1, 1963, a group of South Vietnamese generals led a takeover of their government. Diem and his brother

Nhu surrendered but were shot to death by unidentified killers.

LBJ'S INHERITANCE

South Vietnam's leadership went to General Duong Van Minh. The U.S. leadership was about to shift as well. On November 22, 1963, John F. Kennedy was assassinated while visiting Dallas, Texas. Vice President Lyndon Baines Johnson (LBJ) became the new president. Johnson had vast experience in American politics but little experience in foreign affairs. By this time, more than 15,000 U.S. military advisers were in Vietnam, nine thousand miles from home. President Johnson had inherited a mess.

Ngo Dinh Diem's government arrested Buddhist monks and nuns. His harsh actions led U.S. leaders to abandon their support for Diem.

FROM COLD WAR TO HOT WAR

3

When Lyndon Johnson became president of the United States, conditions in South Vietnam were chaotic. General Minh and other South Vietnamese leaders were too busy arguing with one another to provide leadership for the country. By the end of January 1964, a different general was in charge. Riots and mobs wracked the streets of Saigon. South Vietnam's presidency shifted from one general to another. Meanwhile, the Viet Cong gained strength in the countryside, controlling as much as 45 percent of South Vietnam's territory.

In the summer of 1964, North Vietnam began adding soldiers from its own army to the 50,000 Viet Cong guerrillas in South Vietnam. Thousands of North Vietnamese army "regulars," as these soldiers were known, entered the south secretly along the Ho Chi Minh Trail. The war was heating up.

THE TONKIN INCIDENT

On August 2, 1964, a U.S. warship, the USS *Maddox*, reported being attacked by North Vietnamese patrol boats in the Gulf of Tonkin off the coast of North Vietnam. No Americans were injured. After the incident, President Johnson warned the North Vietnamese not to attack again. On August 4, some crewmembers from the *Maddox* and another warship reported that they were under attack, but they may have been mistaken. Whatever the case, the ships suffered no damage. Yet despite the uncertainty surrounding the events, the

U.S. president decided to strike back at the North Vietnamese.

U.S. planes bombed military installations and oil depots in North Vietnam on August 5. President Johnson said, "[O]ur response for the present will be limited and fitting. We Americans know—although others appear to forget—the risk of spreading conflict. We still seek no wider war." During the bombing raids, two U.S. planes were shot down. One pilot was killed. The other, Lieutenant Everett Alvarez of San Jose, California, became the first American prisoner of war captured by the North Vietnamese.

The U.S. Congress supported President Johnson's reaction to the Gulf of Tonkin incident. On August 7, after the U.S. bombing, Congress passed the Gulf of Tonkin Resolution, which said that

"More Flags"

In April 1964, President Lyndon Johnson asked U.S. allies to participate in the military effort in Vietnam. He said that "more flags" should be represented in the fight against Communism. The response to his request was small. South Korea, Thailand, and Australia sent troops, and the Philippines sent noncombat personnel.

"Congress approves and supports the determination of the President, as Commander in Chief, to take all necessary measures to repel any armed attack against the forces of the United States and to prevent further aggression."

Johnson was elected to his first full term as president on November 3, 1964. During his presidential campaign, he had promised, "We are not going to send American boys nine or ten thousand miles away to do what Asian boys ought to be doing for themselves." But events limited his ability to make good on this promise.

After the U.S. election, the war in South Vietnam worsened. Viet Cong attacked throughout South Vietnam, including attacks aimed at Americans. By December 1964, 10,000 North Vietnamese Army regulars had entered the south along the Ho Chi Minh Trail. Unlike the poorly equipped guerrillas who had come south earlier, the regulars had modern weapons from China and the Soviet Union.

Meanwhile, South Vietnam's leadership continued to teeter. Johnson's new ambassador to Vietnam, General Maxwell Taylor, sent a telegram to Washington, D.C.:

Surrounded by members of Congress, President Lyndon B. Johnson (seated) announces the passing of the Gulf of Tonkin Resolution. The resolution gave Johnson the power to increase the United States' role in Vietnam.

"Only the emergence of an exceptional leader could improve the situation," he wrote, "and no George Washington is in sight."

AMERICA'S AIR WAR

By the end of 1964, roughly 23,000 American military advisers were in Vietnam to train and support the South Vietnamese Army. Yet they were not only training and supporting—some of them were getting killed. The president's aides all agreed the current approach was failing. Some aides favored continued air strikes—bombing raids—against North Vietnam. They also wanted to bomb the Ho Chi Minh Trail, to cut the supply line to the Communist forces.

The Viet Cong helped President Johnson decide what to do. On February 7, 1965, Viet Cong soldiers attacked a U.S. air base near Pleiku in Vietnam's Central Highlands, killing eight Americans. "Cowardice has gotten us into more wars than response has," Johnson told his advisers. Deciding on an aggressive response, he ordered U.S. jets to bomb a North Vietnamese army camp.

President Johnson also agreed to his advisers' recommendation for more air strikes against North Vietnam. Rolling Thunder, as the major bombing campaign was known, began on March 2, 1965.

Rolling Thunder was planned to last two months. In April, however, military advisers told Johnson that the bombing had not yet seriously damaged North Vietnam's ability to wage war. President Johnson ordered the air strikes to continue against military and industrial targets in the north and against the Ho Chi Minh Trail.

A U.S. Air Force F-5 fighter drops its bombs over a target in Vietnam.

At this point, opinion polls showed that 70 percent of the American public supported President Johnson's actions. About 80 percent of Americans believed that a withdrawal of U.S. forces would result in Communist control of Southeast Asia. The same percentage supported sending U.S. combat troops to Vietnam to prevent such a takeover.

SEND IN THE MARINES

The bombing campaign led to another important action—the arrival of U.S. Marines in South Vietnam to protect U.S. airfields there. Lieutenant General William Westmoreland was the U.S. military commander in Vietnam. As he explained, "When the bombing program started, I realized that the airfields—and we had three jet-capable airfields—were extremely vulnerable . . . and therefore, my first request for troops was associated with protecting the airfields."

On March 8, 1965, 3,500 Marine Corps troops started landing on the beach at Da Nang in South Vietnam. They were the first Americans sent to Vietnam who were acknowledged to be combat troops—and they were welcomed ashore by Vietnamese people bearing wreaths of red and yellow flowers. Some held up a poster. It said: "Welcome to the Gallant [brave] Marines."

THE BUILDUP BEGINS

Three weeks after the marines landed, a Viet Cong terrorist exploded a powerful car bomb in front of the U.S. embassy in Saigon. Twenty Vietnamese were killed in the blast, and one hundred thirty wounded.

> **EYEWITNESS QUOTE:**
> **AMERICAN BOMBING RAIDS**
> "You would come back to where your lean-to and bunker had been, your home, and there would simply be nothing there, just an unrecognizable landscape gouged by immense craters."
> —Former Viet Cong official Truong Nhu Tang on the effects of U.S. bombing attacks

U.S. Marines land on the beach at Da Nang. The 3,500 marines were the first official U.S. combat troops to arrive in Vietnam.

Two Americans died, and fifty-two were wounded.

President Johnson's military advisers told him that more troops were necessary for the United States to make a difference in Vietnam. So Johnson sent additional soldiers in the spring of 1965—marines and U.S. Army troops. Along with combat soldiers went logistical troops—soldiers whose job was to support the combat soldiers with medical care, food, equipment, communications, and more. By the summer of 1965, the number of U.S. soldiers in Vietnam had reached 70,000.

Besides increasing the number of U.S. troops in Vietnam, Johnson also changed their mission. In March, when he had sent in the marines, they were charged only with defending American air bases. But soon after their arrival, Johnson authorized General Westmoreland to send Americans into combat—to go on the offensive to find and kill the Viet Cong.

In June 1965, General Nguyen Van Thieu and Air Marshal Nguyen Cao Ky formed a new government in South Vietnam. Ky was a showy young South Vietnamese air force officer. Thieu had once been a member of the Viet Minh before joining the French-created Vietnamese Army. General Westmoreland reported that soldiers in the South Vietnamese Army were deserting—quitting the army without permission—at a high rate. He called for more U.S. reinforcement—as many as 200,000 troops by the end of 1965, and another 100,000 in 1966—to support the South Vietnamese regime.

Westmoreland's bold requests led to serious debate in Washington, D.C. President

Lyndon B. Johnson

Johnson was deeply worried about where the buildup would end. According to presidential aide Jack Valenti, Johnson said, "What happens if in two, three, four years you ask me for 500,000 men?"

Yet Johnson agreed to send General Westmoreland 175,000 soldiers in 1965. "I have asked the commanding general, General Westmoreland, what more he needs to meet this mounting aggression," Johnson said at a press conference. "He has told me. And we will meet his needs."

The decision to send more troops was a turning point. The conflict in Vietnam was not going to be won by U.S. pilots dropping bombs on distant targets. U.S. combat troops would be slogging it out on the ground.

BE PROUD OF ME

The escalation of the war created controversy in the United States and in other countries. On October 16, 1965, antiwar demonstrations took place in forty cities across the United States and in Europe. Many of the American protesters were college students who were eligible to be drafted (enrolled) for military service. As more protests took place, many young protesters burned their draft cards—cards issued by the government that showed they were registered for the draft—at antiwar rallies. By doing this, they risked fines or imprisonment. Still, the majority of the American public supported Johnson's decisions about the war at this time.

HARDWARE AND ARMAMENTS

U.S. FORCES

B-52 bombers High-altitude jets used to bomb North Vietnam and the Ho Chi Minh Trail
• Payload up to 100 bombs
• Other bombers included F-105 Thunderchiefs, A-4 Skyhawks, and A-1 Skyraiders

B-52

Fighter planes High-speed attack aircraft, launched from aircraft carriers or from land bases. Often used for ground assault or against enemy aircraft.
• F-4 Phantom, widely used, armed with 20-millimeter cannons and air-to-air missiles
• F-5 Freedom Fighter, armed with cannon and missiles. Carried up to 5,500 pounds of bombs.

Bell UH-1 helicopters ("Hueys") All-purpose helicopters—carried troops and equipment, evacuated wounded and dead, and used as gunship with added weapons such as machine guns and rocket or grenade launchers. Could carry eight soldiers.

CH-47 (Chinook) Large helicopter with double rotors, used to move large artillery, ammunition, and troops. Could carry twenty-five soldiers.

Napalm Usually dropped in canisters from aircraft. Sticky gel caused targets—including people—to burst into flames

M-16 rifles Standard weapon carried by U.S. ground troops
• On automatic setting, fired 750 to 900 rounds (bullets) per minute
• Soldiers carried clips of 20 or 30 rounds
• Range of 1,300 feet

M-16

Grenades Hand-held explosive devices carried by ground troops
• To use a grenade, a soldier threw it after removing the fuse pin
• Other types were shot using a launcher
• Fragmentation grenades burst into metal fragments when detonated

Claymore Mines Antipersonnel device—designed to injure or kill people
• Often buried in ground and rigged to set off when the target made contact with it
• Could also be triggered by trip wire, stumbled over by an enemy, or pulled by a concealed U.S. soldier
• Explosion released hundreds of metal pieces that traveled as far as 150 feet

VIET CONG AND NORTH VIETNAMESE FORCES

MiG-21 fighter jets Soviet-built high-altitude jets, often used against U.S. fighters
• Equipped with 30-millimeter cannon and air-to-air missiles
• Reached speeds up to 1,300 miles per hour

130-millimeter howitzer Large cannons that were towed into position
• Range of 71,000 feet

Antiaircraft missiles Used to shoot down planes and helicopters
• SA7 Grail, portable antiaircraft weapon

Tanks T-54/55 tanks manufactured in the Soviet Union
• 100-millimeter turret-mounted main
  gun; machine gun

AK-47 rifles Common
rifle among Communist
troops, supplied by China and
Soviet Union

AK-47

• Fired rounds at rate up to 600 per minute
• Ammunition carried in clips of 30 rounds
• Range more than 1,300 feet

Mines and anti-personnel weapons Chinese and Soviet-supplied or
homemade by Viet Cong using discarded American ammunition, batteries, and even
food containers

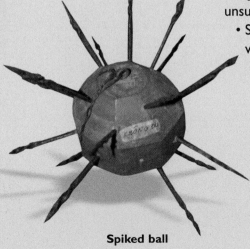

Booby traps Devices rigged to cause injury to
unsuspecting enemies
• Spiked balls hung from trees, triggered by trip
  wires
• Punji pit—a hole in the ground in which
  fire-hardened bamboo stakes, called punji
  sticks, were hidden to pierce the feet of
  unsuspecting victims
• Punji sticks were sometimes poisoned with
  human or animal excrement to create
  infected wounds

Spiked ball

While doubts and protests gathered strength at home, many—perhaps even most—American soldiers in Vietnam believed they were fighting for a worthwhile cause.

Richard E. Marks, a marine private, wrote to his mother on December 12, 1965, "I am fighting to protect and maintain what I believe in and what I want to live in—a democratic society. If I am killed while carrying out this mission, I want no one to cry or mourn for me. I want people to hold their heads high and be proud of me for the job I did."

Richard Marks was killed in Vietnam on February 14, 1966. He was nineteen.

The Draft

One way in which young men found out if they had been drafted was through a lottery system. During a lottery drawing *(above)*, slips of paper with birth dates were pulled. Every birth date was given a number, based on the order in which it had been drawn. Draft-eligible young men were called to duty according to the number assigned to their birth dates.

The U.S. government relied on a process called the draft to provide men for war. By law, all men in the United States were required to register with an agency called the Selective Service System upon their eighteenth birthday. Selective Service classified each young man in one of several categories, from 1-A (available for military service) to 4-F (not qualified for service because of, for example, a medical problem). Selective Service also created categories for conscientious objectors —individuals who claimed that military service would violate their religious or ethical beliefs. Depending on the nation's needs, the Selective Service issued draft calls each month— requiring a number of qualified men to report for military service. In the summer of 1965, for example, the draft calls were 35,000 men per month. Men could be drafted until they turned twenty-six.

Category 2-S—deferment (delaying service) due to college studies—allowed many young men to avoid service in Vietnam. But young men who could not afford college could not take advantage of the student deferment.

Draft evasion was a major problem. To avoid the draft, some young men did not register on their eighteenth birthday. Others ignored the draft notices the Selective Service sent to tell them to report for duty. Some young men, with assistance from sympathetic doctors, lied about medical conditions to qualify as 4-F. Others fled to Canada or other countries.

AMERICANS
4 AT WAR

With so many American combat troops "in country" (in Vietnam), the nature of the war changed. American soldiers no longer waited for combat to happen to them. They sought out fights. In other, more traditional wars, such as World War II, enemy armies faced off in large battles. The enemies usually met at a front, or front line—in a major line of battle. But the Viet Cong used guerrilla tactics, so U.S. soldiers often could not find them to fight them. As Vietnam veteran (ex-soldier) Bernard Edelman explained, "In the guerrilla war that was Vietnam there was no 'front'. . . . So the grunts [ground troops] humped, sweeping through the countryside on search-and-

destroy operations, setting up ambushes, seeking to make contact with an elusive enemy, the Viet Cong . . . and the NVA—the North Vietnamese Army."

IA DRANG

Yet some large, more traditional battles did occur. The first major battle in this beefed-up war occurred at the Ia Drang Valley. In October 1965, North Vietnamese troops gathered near the valley in South Vietnam's Central Highlands. They seemed to be preparing a takeover of the highlands region. On October 19, they attacked a U.S. Army Special Forces camp in Plei Me—and then disappeared. U.S. troops staged a major operation against the North Vietnamese forces a few weeks later, on November 14. Dropped by helicopters into a landing zone code-named LZ X-RAY, American soldiers fought a tough battle with the Communist troops. Heavy U.S. artillery fire and air strikes provided added firepower.

After two days of intense fighting, the North Vietnamese retreated. Although reports of casualties (the dead, wounded, captured, and missing) varied, the Americans said that more than 1,500 Communist soldiers had been killed in the battle of Ia Drang, compared to fewer than 300 Americans.

Ia Drang was an American victory. But it was an alarming victory, for the battle showed that there were far more North Vietnamese soldiers in the south than first thought. With this new information, General Westmoreland sent a message to Washington, D.C., in late 1965. He wanted 200,000 more American troops in 1966—twice the number he had asked for earlier.

SEARCH AND DESTROY

President Johnson did not agree to Westmoreland's request right away. Instead, the president paused Rolling Thunder, hoping to make peace with North Vietnam. The Communists did not respond to his call for discussions. In the spring of 1966, President Johnson decided to send General Westmoreland the 200,000 soldiers he had asked for.

U.S. marines walk through fields of rice on a search-and-destroy mission.

Agent Orange

U.S. and South Vietnamese military leaders were frustrated by the Viet Cong's ability to launch attacks from hidden positions in South Vietnam's jungles. To eliminate these hiding places, in 1962 the United States started spraying areas of jungle with an herbicide—a plant-destroying chemical—known as Agent Orange. The colorless substance took its name from an orange stripe painted on its storage containers. For eight years, U.S. planes sprayed thousands of square miles of jungle.

After the war ended, many U.S. soldiers who had been in Vietnam developed illnesses such as cancers, liver disease, and skin rashes. They believed their illnesses resulted from exposure to Agent Orange. U.S. military and government agencies conducted studies to determine if these claims were true. The studies could not prove or disprove the claims. Many Vietnamese also suffered health problems that they say stemmed from Agent Orange.

Thousands of Vietnam veterans sued the chemical companies that produced Agent Orange during the war. The companies eventually agreed to settle the lawsuits by paying money to sick veterans and creating an organization to help veterans and their families.

In 1966 U.S. troops began major search-and-destroy missions against the North Vietnamese and Viet Cong in South Vietnam. During these missions, large numbers of helicopters transported U.S. troops to a landing zone. From the landing zone, the soldiers searched for the enemy—who might be hiding in a jungle or a stream valley or a rice paddy (field)—and fought them. At the end of the fight, the American soldiers usually moved on or flew back to a base. In smaller patrols, American soldiers moved by foot into villages and other places to capture or kill Viet Cong hiding there. Again, after the mission, the Americans left.

BIGGER TARGETS— CEDAR FALLS AND JUNCTION CITY

By early 1967, the United States had 400,000 troops in Vietnam. Communist forces in the south numbered nearly 300,000, according to U.S. military estimates. Search and destroy remained the U.S. military strategy, but with a new focus. In future missions, U.S. soldiers would not merely kill the Viet Cong. They were to destroy their means of getting food and weapons. U.S. forces also tried to separate the enemy from South Vietnamese villagers who might be helping them.

SOLDIERS

U.S. Soldiers

General William Westmoreland in his U.S. Army officer's uniform

U.S. soldiers who served in Vietnam went through a wide variety of experiences. Some inched their way through jungle thickets. There they met the Viet Cong in ferocious bursts of combat. Other troops guarded the areas around American camps. These men often encountered gunfire from hidden Viet Cong or North Vietnamese snipers (hidden enemy shooters). Pilots risked their lives flying over enemy territory. There they faced hostile fire, dropping their deadly bombs over North Vietnam.

Soldiers' training also varied, depending on their branch of the military service—army, marines, navy, or air force. In general, troops went through basic training. They were put through a physical training program. They learned how to operate weapons and carry out military maneuvers.

Although their duties and experiences differed, most U.S. servicemen shared a common attitude in the early years of the war. They generally believed that their work in Vietnam was important to South Vietnam, the United States, and the free world at large. By 1968, as the war lost the support of Americans back home, morale declined. As it became clear that the United States was not fighting to win, many soldiers became more concerned with surviving their tour of duty in Vietnam than with victory.

American Uniforms

An army combat soldier was issued pants and a shirt of olive green fabric and a steel helmet. Although the helmets provided protection from bullets and flying shrapnel, they were uncomfortable in the hot climate. Many soldiers did not wear them. The uniforms were more comfortable. But some soldiers still adopted the loose, thin pants worn by native Vietnamese. On their feet, soldiers wore jungle boots designed to help prevent "immersion foot"—a condition caused by constantly wet feet. These boots had reinforced soles to protect against punji sticks. Rounding out the typical uniform was a web belt with pouches for ammunition, a first aid kit, and one or more canteens. A soldier might also drape belts of ammunition around his neck.

Viet Cong and North Vietnamese Soldiers

Viet Cong and North Vietnamese troops operated under stealth conditions. This meant they kept out of sight in the South Vietnamese and nearby Cambodian jungles. They came out of hiding to attack U.S. or South Vietnamese positions—and then they faded back into the jungle again. Some were full-time, uniformed soldiers. Others were part-timers. Some were highly motivated volunteers, while others were forced to fight.

The life of a full-time guerrilla was grueling. "We lived like hunted animals, an existence that demanded constant physical and mental alertness," said Truong Nhu Tang, a former Viet Cong leader. Guerrillas traveled light. They carried only a few supplies: weapons, ammunition, and food. Sometimes soldiers would hunt elephants, tigers, monkeys, and even wild dogs to eat.

A North Vietnamese soldier in officer's uniform

Soldiers who joined larger Viet Cong or North Vietnamese units received instruction in guerrilla warfare methods. Guerrilla training centers were hidden throughout the South Vietnamese countryside. An important part of training for all soldiers was political instruction. Communist leaders appointed political officers, or cadres, even to small military units, to provide instruction on Communist principles.

Viet Cong and North Vietnamese Uniforms

Viet Cong guerrillas who lived among civilians in South Vietnam wore clothes that allowed them to blend in with their neighbors. Most wore black pajama-like pants and shirts. Members of the North Vietnamese Army wore green uniforms. Some wore helmets made of pressed paper and plastic to protect them from the sun. On their feet, some North Vietnamese troops wore cloth jungle boots. However, the weather and landscape caused boots to wear out quickly. Many soldiers adopted the Viet Cong's sandals with soles made from tire treads. North Vietnamese Army soldiers were issued a canvas belt, with pouches for canteens, grenades, and ammunition. They carried backpacks for additional gear or supplies.

The new goals meant new complications. U.S. or South Vietnamese troops sometimes attacked South Vietnamese citizens who were thought to be siding with the Viet Cong. Since the Viet Cong did not wear uniforms and could be men, women, or even children, it was often impossible to know for sure who was Viet Cong and who was not. Many innocents were killed. The United States was fighting a kind of warfare it had never fought before. Although the United States had more soldiers and better weapons and equipment, it could not crush an enemy that it could not always find.

On January 8, 1967, American and South Vietnamese soldiers launched Operation Cedar Falls, a major search-and-destroy operation twenty-five miles northwest of Saigon. The target was an area known as the Iron Triangle. The Viet Cong and the NLF had a major base in the Iron Triangle. Local villagers gave them food and shelter. The Viet Cong had also dug a huge web of underground tunnels in the area. There, under the earth's surface, the Viet Cong hid from attackers in these tunnels and stored huge quantities of ammunition and food. They had stashed enough rice, according to U.S. Air Force colonel and Vietnam veteran Gene Gurney, to feed 13,000 soldiers for one year.

Operation Cedar Falls lasted three weeks. Yet the mission did not involve traditional combat. As U.S. forces approached, the Viet Cong abandoned the tunnels and disappeared into the jungle. Thus the Americans were not able to kill many Viet Cong fighters. Instead, the U.S. and South Vietnamese forces evacuated, or removed, the people who lived in the area and destroyed their villages.

Operation Cedar Falls was designed to destroy Viet Cong hideouts. Here bamboo huts go up in flames during a U.S. Army attack on a Viet Cong stronghold.

The Underground War

The Viet Cong and North Vietnamese needed bases and camps in South Vietnam where soldiers could meet and train. But such bases had to be hidden from the Americans. To solve this problem, the Communist fighters built complex systems of underground tunnels. These tunnels served as passageways beneath aboveground facilities. They could be used to escape if the bases were discovered or came under attack. The tunnels also contained underground storage rooms for food and weapons, weapons factories, sleeping chambers, hospitals, and kitchens. Smoke from the kitchens' stoves was directed sideways into the earth so that escaping smoke would not give away the guerrillas' location. The bases ranged in size, but the big ones were very big. At Cu Chi, only twenty miles from Saigon, the Viet Cong maintained a base with nearly seventy-five miles of underground tunnels.

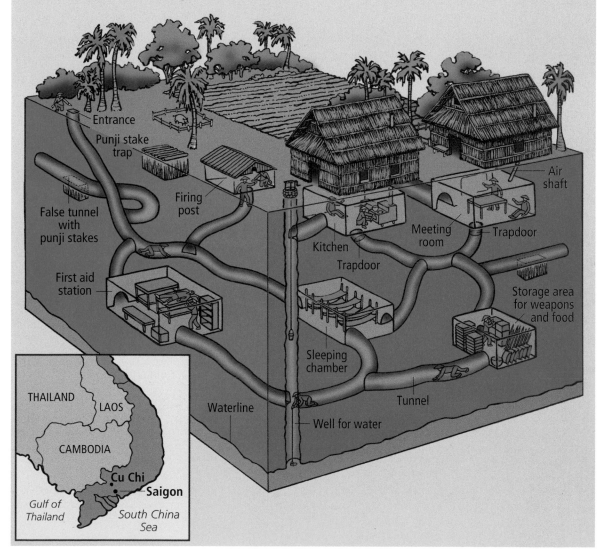

Entrance

Punji stake trap

Firing post

False tunnel with punji stakes

First aid station

Kitchen

Trapdoor

Meeting room

Trapdoor

Air shaft

Storage area for weapons and food

Sleeping chamber

Tunnel

Waterline

Well for water

THAILAND

LAOS

CAMBODIA

Cu Chi

Saigon

Gulf of Thailand

South China Sea

Another, even larger search-and-destroy mission, called Operation Junction City, began on February 22, 1967. American and South Vietnamese troops attacked North Vietnamese Army and Viet Cong bases northwest of Saigon, trying to destroy the Communists' headquarters in the south. This time, the fighting was intense. For the first time in the war, U.S. troops parachuted into combat. They pursued Communist soldiers trying to escape into Cambodia. Junction City lasted until May 14. Nearly 300 U.S. soldiers were killed. By an American count, 3,000 Viet Cong died in the operation.

American officials pronounced Cedar Falls and Junction City successful operations. In both, the enemy left the targeted areas. But in a pattern that repeated itself throughout the war, the Viet Cong made their way back to the destroyed areas after U.S. forces withdrew. By the end of 1967, the Iron Triangle was once again filled with Viet Cong, busy rebuilding the bases destroyed by the Americans.

DISCOURAGING RESULTS

The results of the U.S. fighting and bombings in 1966 and 1967 were not as good as military leaders had hoped. North Vietnamese combat troops were still making their way south in large numbers and leading much of the fighting in the south. Rolling Thunder was causing destruction in the north, but it was not hurting the Communists' ability to fight in the south. This was mainly because China and the Soviet Union supplied the North Vietnamese with arms and equipment. Chinese troops also rebuilt North Vietnamese railroad tracks, bridges, and roads damaged by U.S. bombs. Yet U.S. leaders were unwilling to attack supply routes from the Soviets and Chinese. They feared that such moves would lead to a massive worldwide war.

U.S. troops drop into a landing zone near Cambodia during Operation Junction City. Helicopters provided fast access to and from battle areas.

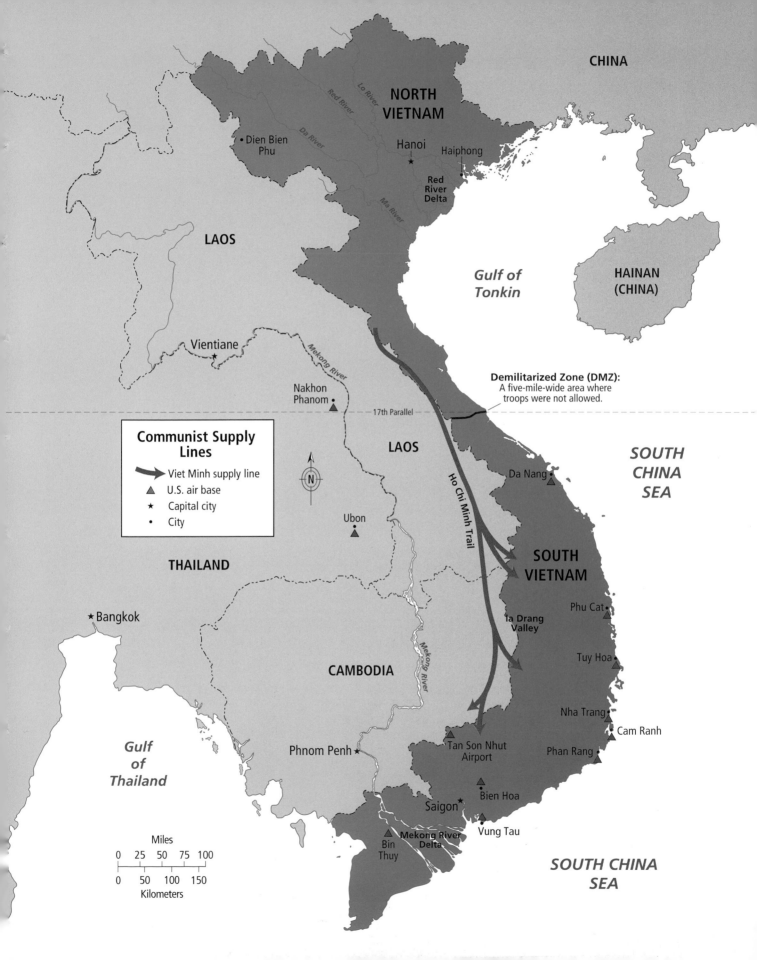

CHINA

NORTH
VIETNAM

Dien Bien
Phu

Red River
Lo River
Da River

Hanoi

Haiphong

Red
River
Delta

Ma River

LAOS

Gulf of
Tonkin

HAINAN
(CHINA)

Vientiane

Mekong River

Nakhon
Phanom

17th Parallel

Demilitarized Zone (DMZ):
A five-mile-wide area where
troops were not allowed.

**Communist Supply
Lines**

➤ Viet Minh supply line
▲ U.S. air base
★ Capital city
• City

LAOS

SOUTH
CHINA
SEA

Da Nang

N

Ubon

Ho Chi Minh Trail

SOUTH
VIETNAM

THAILAND

Phu Cat

Ia Drang
Valley

Tuy Hoa

★ Bangkok

CAMBODIA

Mekong River

Nha Trang

Cam Ranh

Gulf
of
Thailand

Phnom Penh ★

Tan Son Nhut
Airport

Phan Rang

Bien Hoa

Saigon ★

Miles

0 25 50 75 100

Vung Tau

0   50   100   150
Kilometers

Bin
Thuy

Mekong River
Delta

SOUTH CHINA
SEA

In the south, the U.S. troops had little success against the enemy. Civilians—not Viet Cong soldiers—seemed to suffer the most. According to Secretary of Defense Robert McNamara, between 1965 and 1967, the U.S. and South Vietnamese militaries dropped more than one million tons of bombs on the south—twice the amount dropped on the north during that period. As many as four million people—one-quarter of the population of South Vietnam—left their bombed-out homes in the country to find safety in cities and towns. Many moved to crowded refugee camps, where deadly diseases were common. Others took to the streets in cities such as Saigon and Da Nang, begging or becoming involved in crime.

General Westmoreland asked for 200,000 more soldiers in 1967, seeking to raise the total of U.S. forces in Vietnam to 670,000. (President Johnson had already authorized up to 470,000.) In late 1967, Westmoreland told a group of journalists, "We have reached an important point, when the end begins to come into view." He also said, "Everybody is very optimistic that I know of, who is intimately associated with our effort there."

Yet many U.S. policymakers and other leaders were not optimistic at all. In April 1967, civil rights leader Martin Luther King Jr. gave a major speech criticizing Johnson's war policies. Democratic senator Robert F. Kennedy, brother of the late President Kennedy, criticized U.S. actions in Vietnam. Democratic senator Eugene McCarthy announced in November 1967 that he would run as an antiwar candidate for president in 1968. Republican Ronald Reagan, governor of California, also opposed U.S. involvement in Vietnam. Reagan was not antiwar, but he believed U.S. decisions to limit the war made victory nearly impossible.

Ordinary Americans were also frustrated. Many took to the streets in 1967 to protest the U.S. escalation—the expansion of the war. According to an October 1967 survey, support for the war in Vietnam had dropped. Forty-six percent of Americans believed that U.S. military involvement in Vietnam was wrong.

Many protesters called the war in Vietnam "McNamara's War," referring to Secretary of Defense Robert McNamara, who at first had supported the war. Yet even he was changing his mind. In May 1967, McNamara told President Johnson that escalation was not working and that Johnson should refuse General Westmoreland's request for more new troops. He suggested less bombing and stronger attempts to negotiate with the North Vietnamese.

The president and his other military advisers did not accept McNamara's outlook. Although Johnson was not willing to send General Westmoreland 200,000 additional troops, he also was not willing to pull back. He agreed to send 45,000 more American soldiers to Vietnam.

On November 29, 1967, Robert McNamara announced his resignation as secretary of defense. He wanted no more of the Vietnam War.

Robert McNamara

5 TURNING POINT

By the middle of 1967, the Communists were planning major attacks against the south. Their goal was to set the stage for an outright invasion by North Vietnamese troops in 1968.

On January 21, 1968, North Vietnam launched a major assault on the U.S. air base at Khe Sanh, near the border between North and South Vietnam. The Communist troops circled the base, which housed nearly 6,000 U.S. Marines. The attack turned into a siege. Under heavy fire from North Vietnamese artillery, the marines held off the attackers. But the U.S. forces could not push them back.

Weeks passed, and the marines at Khe Sanh grew short of supplies. To loosen the Communists' grip, U.S. B-52 bombers rained down 100,000 tons of bombs on the attackers. After seventy-seven days, the North Vietnamese gave up their hold on Khe Sanh. The siege was broken on April 8, 1968.

Two hundred marines died holding on to the air base. Yet just months later, U.S. military leaders closed down the base at Khe Sanh. Close to the North Vietnamese border and far from other U.S. positions, the base was vulnerable to attack. Although Khe Sanh was potentially useful as a launching pad for attacks on the North Vietnamese, by spring of 1968, the United States was not interested in expanding the war through such attacks.

The Rats of Khe Sanh

The U.S. soldiers surrounded at Khe Sanh had to fight more than the North Vietnamese. They had another enemy: rats. The air base had always had a rat problem, but it worsened with the siege. As a *Time* magazine article reported, "Rats became frantic under fire. When incoming [fire] starts, the rats race for the bunkers and wildly run up to the ceilings made of runway matting and logs. One sergeant killed thirty-four rats, establishing a base record."

THE TET OFFENSIVE

In late January, ten days after the assault on Khe Sanh began, the North Vietnamese launched an even bigger attack on South Vietnam's cities. The South Vietnamese and Viet Cong had made a truce, an agreement not to fight, during Tet, the Vietnamese New Year celebration. Viet Cong and North Vietnamese troops used the lull in the fighting to secretly move into cities, towns, and villages all over South Vietnam.

In Saigon the Tet celebrations provided cover for thousands of Viet Cong, who sneaked into the city disguised as ordinary citizens. As National Liberation Front member Tong Viet Duong told an interviewer, "Taxis carried chrysanthemums [flowers] into Saigon for the Tet market. Hidden underneath them were AK-47s [rifles]. . . . We changed our clothes and carried fake identity documents. The people of Saigon hid us in their houses."

On January 31, 1968, the Communists struck. As many as 84,000 Viet Cong and North Vietnamese troops attacked Saigon and dozens of other cities, towns, villages, air bases, and other targets. This huge operation came to be known as the Tet Offensive.

The streets of Saigon became a battleground during the Tet Offensive in January–February 1968.

CHINA

NORTH
VIETNAM

Red River

• Dien Bien
Phu

Hanoi ★

Haiphong

LAOS

Gulf of
Tonkin

HAINAN
(CHINA)

Vientiane •

Mekong River

THAILAND

17th Parallel

DMZ

Quang Tri
Hue
Phu Loc
Da Nang
Tam Ky
Chu Lai

Phu
Bai

Hoi An

SOUTH
CHINA
SEA

**The Tet Offensive Begins
January 31, 1968**

Communist attack

Viet Minh supply line

Military base

★ Capital city

• City

N

LAOS

Ho Chi Minh Trail

Bong Son

Kontum

Pleiku   Ankhe   Qui Nhon

Hau Bon   Tuy Hoa

Ban Me Thuot

Nha Trang

Da Lat

Phan Rang

★Bangkok

CAMBODIA

Mekong River

Phnom Penh ★

Tay
Ninh

Phu
Cuong

SOUTH
VIETNAM

Duc Hoa

Bien Hoa

Gulf
of
Thailand

Cha Phu

Mo
Hoa

Gia Dinh

Saigon

Phan Thiet

Phuoc Le

Sa Dec

My Tho

Rach Gia

Ben Tre

Phu Vinh

Can Tho

Bac Lieu   Vinh Long

Soc Trang

Ca Mau

SOUTH
CHINA
SEA

Miles

0   25   50   75   100

0   50   100   150

Kilometers

In most places, U.S. and South Vietnamese soldiers quickly pushed back the attackers. But in the coastal city of Hue, the Communists gained control and held the city for nearly a month. During that time, Communist soldiers hunted down people who supported the South Vietnamese government and killed them. The victims included merchants, clergymen, government employees, and military officers. Three thousand people were murdered. The event came to be known as the Hue Massacre. On February 24, 1968, U.S. and South Vietnamese troops recaptured Hue.

The fight cost the lives of more than 500 Americans and South Vietnamese soldiers. As many as 5,000 Viet Cong and North Vietnamese were killed.

VICTORY TO THE LOSER

The Tet offensive was a military loss for the North Vietnamese and Viet Cong. About 4,300 South Vietnamese and Americans died, compared to 45,000 Viet Cong and North Vietnamese. The Communists had hoped that many South Vietnamese would join the fight against the U.S. troops and the South Vietnamese government, easing the way for a final North Vietnamese invasion. But Tet did not lead to a massive surge of support for the Communists in South Vietnam.

U.S. marines on the streets of Hue during the Tet Offensive. Retaking the city from Communist forces involved house-to-house fighting. By the end of the battle, nearly half the city lay in ruins.

Despite the Communist defeat, many Americans came to believe that the United States could not win the war in Vietnam. Three years of bombing and search-and-destroy missions had not stopped the Communists from launching a large-scale, well-planned operation. General Westmoreland's optimistic reports were being questioned. The end was not coming into view, as he had said it would a few months earlier. The Communists were not on the verge of defeat. Instead, Tet proved they were ready to go on fighting indefinitely.

As reporter Jonathan Schell wrote, "the Vietnam war was a war for time, and in the war for time what our foe [enemy] had to do was not win battles but demonstrate that it could endure defeats. At Tet, the foe demonstrated its endurance beyond a shadow of a doubt, and in a way that the whole world could see and understand. It did this not by winning any battle but by launching the attack in the first place."

Clark Clifford, a well-known lawyer in Washington, D.C., replaced Robert McNamara as secretary of defense. After Tet, he met in March 1968 with the Joint Chiefs of Staff—the heads of each branch of the U.S. military. He soon realized that the leaders did not know what it would take to win the war. They did not know how many more American soldiers and how much time would be needed to do the job. Clifford did not think the United States could continue to fight a war in such a state of uncertainty. "The time has come to decide where we go from here," he told President Johnson.

Some military advisers thought the United States should expand the bombing

Charting the War of Attrition

In a war without front lines, killing the enemy was more important than controlling an area. The conflict became a war of attrition—of slowly chipping away at the opponent's strength and numbers. Success was measured by the number of enemy soldiers killed.

For a period of time, U.S. military leaders ordered combat soldiers to produce daily body counts—the number of enemy killed. According to many troops, the numbers were often exaggerated. The count of the enemy dead frequently included all Vietnamese who had died, including noncombatants, women, children, and old men.

"[T]hey had a habit of exaggerating a body count," said U.S. Army combat engineer Harold Bryant. "If we killed 7, by the time it would get back to base camp, it would have gotten to 28. Then by the time it got down to Westmoreland's office in Saigon, it . . . went up to 54. And by the time it left Saigon going to Washington, it . . . [was] about 125. To prove we were really out there doing our jobs, doing, really, more than what we were doing."

of North Vietnam. General Westmoreland also asked for 200,000 more troops, on top of the 500,000 already in Vietnam. But President Johnson was losing faith in Westmoreland, and soon replaced him as commander of the Vietnam conflict with General Creighton Abrams.

Other advisers disagreed with these strategies. Some thought the bombing should be stopped. They hoped this would convince the North Vietnamese to talk peace. These decisions were left to the president and commander in chief, Lyndon Johnson.

WOMEN IN THE VIETNAM WAR

Ninety percent of the 11,000 American women who served in Vietnam were military nurses. Approximately 1,200 served in other jobs. These included communications specialists, translators, air traffic controllers, photographers, typists, and clerks.

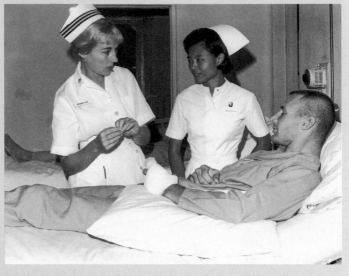

An American and a Thai nurse comfort a patient in a Saigon hospital.

Before heading to Vietnam, women went through basic military training in the United States. Despite this training, U.S. policy was not to issue weapons to women in Vietnam, since they were noncombatants.

Yet women were certainly exposed to hostilities. Precilla Wilkewitz worked in the army's inspector general's office in Long Binh in 1968 and 1969. She told a reporter, "We had mortar attacks that could have landed on our compound and killed all of us. Did we have anything to protect us? No, all we had was prayer. And I did a lot of that."

Unlike men, women were not subject to the military draft. Many volunteered for service in Vietnam. Jacqueline Navarra Rhoads, in Vietnam between 1970 and 1971, worked mostly at a surgical hospital in Quang Tri. "I know it sounds crazy—but I wanted to do something for my country," she said.

Eight American women died in Vietnam. Sharon Lane, an army lieutenant and nurse, was the only U.S. servicewoman killed by hostile fire. She was killed during a rocket attack after tending to Vietnamese patients in the prisoner ward at Chu Lai hospital.

On the Viet Cong and North Vietnamese side of the war, women served in large numbers. They worked in support positions and also as soldiers. Young women worked on the Ho Chi Minh Trail as members of repair crews. These crews patched up the trail after U.S. bombing raids. Many women served as nurses. Others were guerrilla fighters. Women were also members of the Viet Cong's "shadow government" in South Vietnam—including Dr. Duong Quynh Hoa, minister of health. Hoa gave birth to a baby boy in the Cambodian jungle while fleeing an expected U.S. attack. The baby later died of malaria.

AFRICAN AMERICANS IN THE VIETNAM WAR

African Americans served as ground troops, paratroopers, pilots, sailors, engineers, and in other jobs in Vietnam. Many found that the demands of combat erased color differences and racism among soldiers. Charles Strong was an army machine gunner in 1969 and 1970. He told author Wallace Terry, "When I was in the field, they had no room for racism at all. Maybe someone would first come in with it, but after a while, he knew that you were working together as a unit and he needed each man."

Yet African American soldiers also experienced bigotry. If racism was hard to find in the field, where combat went on, it was strong in the "back"—at base camps and installations away from the fighting. Many African Americans felt that their white commanding officers were more likely to send black soldiers than white soldiers into dangerous combat. They also found themselves assigned to dirty, unpleasant jobs, such as cleaning duties on an army base or laundry on a navy ship, more often than seemed fair.

Black soldiers fought in Vietnam at a time when many African Americans were fighting for equal rights and opportunities at home. When black veterans came home from Vietnam, they sometimes encountered disrespect and anger from other African Americans. Those who criticized black soldiers believed that black people should not have been fighting a war against another people of color, the Vietnamese.

Despite these pressures, African Americans served bravely in the war. One soldier who fought in Vietnam later became the first African American chairman of the Joint Chiefs of Staff (the president's top military adviser) and the first African American secretary of state: General Colin Powell.

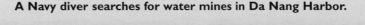

A Navy diver searches for water mines in Da Nang Harbor.

JOHNSON'S SURPRISE ANNOUNCEMENT

For three years, Johnson had agonized over his military decisions. He repeatedly said he hated to send American troops to Vietnam. "We would rather show Hanoi how to grow better rice and how to let its people learn to read and get happy," he told *New York Times* reporter C. L. Sulzberger. "They can do all that the day they stop fighting. We are not declaring war; we are declaring peace."

Yet although Johnson hated sending America's young men to die, he also hated to lose. He could not stand the idea that the United States—and he, personally— might appear weak. He didn't want the world to think the United States didn't fulfill its commitments. And the United States had committed itself to keeping South Vietnam a non-Communist nation. At the same time, Johnson was unwilling to start a full-scale war against the Communists. He was not willing to invade North Vietnam and destroy its ability to wage war against the south. Johnson feared such actions would ignite war with the Soviet Union and China.

But the conflict in Vietnam was dividing the American public. And it was making Johnson highly unpopular. Public opinion polls taken after Tet showed only

My Lai, March 16, 1968

On March 16, 1968, soldiers under the command of U.S. Army Lieutenant William L. Calley Jr. rounded up and killed more than 300 unarmed South Vietnamese civilians in the South Vietnamese village of My Lai. Members of Calley's platoon said that Calley had ordered them to kill the civilians—including old men, women, and children who were pleading for their lives—at close range. Not all of the soldiers took part in the massacre. Some civilians survived by hiding under the dead bodies of neighbors and relatives.

The army charged Calley with murder and prosecuted him in a court-martial, a special military criminal trial. Calley insisted that he only meant to protect his men's lives from the Viet Cong. A jury of military officers did not accept Calley's explanation. In March 1971, he was convicted of first-degree murder and sentenced to life in prison. President Nixon reduced the sentence to twenty years and allowed Calley to serve the sentence under house arrest (under guard in his own house, instead of in prison). In November 1974, a federal judge overturned the conviction on legal grounds, and Calley was freed.

Many war veterans found the My Lai massacre inexcusable, but they also understood how it could have happened. The enemy was difficult to identify to begin with. And U.S. soldiers also had a mission that made it hard to know what was right or wrong. As Fred Widmer, a radio operator in My Lai, said, "Our mission was not to win terrain or territory or seize positions, but simply to kill; to kill Communists and to kill as many of them as possible. . . . It is not surprising, therefore, that some men acquired a contempt for human life and a predilection [preference] for taking it."

26 percent of people surveyed approved of Johnson's handling of the war. Senators Eugene McCarthy and Robert F. Kennedy were challenging Johnson to become the Democratic Party's candidate for the presidency in the November 1968 election.

On March 31, 1968, President Johnson appeared on national television. He had made his decisions. First, the bombing campaign against North Vietnam was to be sharply reduced. Second, he would send only a small number of additional U.S. troops—13,500—to Vietnam. This was far fewer than the 206,000 requested.

"I call upon President Ho Chi Minh to respond positively, and favorably, to this new step toward peace," Johnson said.

Then Johnson made a further announcement. It surprised even his friends. "I shall not seek, and I will not accept, the nomination of my party for another term as your president."

TALKING PEACE, MAKING WAR

Three days after Johnson's speech, the North Vietnamese agreed to hold peace talks. Ironically, these moves toward peace were followed by increased fighting. In May the North Vietnamese and Viet Cong launched another major offensive across South Vietnam.

On May 10, peace talks began in Paris. The United States insisted that North Vietnam remove its troops from the south. This was unacceptable to the Communists. The Communists insisted that the Viet Cong be included in the government of South Vietnam. This was unacceptable to the Americans and to South Vietnamese president Nguyen Van Thieu.

Nguyen Van Thieu was the president of South Vietnam during the 1968 peace talks.

The peace talks stalled almost as soon as they had started.

On November 1, 1968, President Johnson ended Rolling Thunder completely. After three years and eight months, the American air bombing campaign against North Vietnam was stopped. By taking this step, LBJ hoped to spur on the stalled Paris peace talks.

The halt to the bombing was also due to U.S. politics. Americans held hundreds of protests against the war in 1968. In August at the national convention of the Democratic Party in Chicago, Illinois, protesters had gathered outside the convention hall. The protest turned violent. About 26,000

police and members of the National Guard fought with antiwar protesters. The scene was broadcast live on television to a horrified nation.

Johnson had thought the termination of Rolling Thunder might help the presidential candidate he supported, his vice president, Hubert Humphrey. Democrat Humphrey faced Republican Richard Nixon in the election. Nixon pledged to bring "an honorable end to the war in Vietnam." To many Americans, this was a welcome message. They wanted a change. The violent protests at the Democratic convention in Chicago had also turned many people against the Democrats. On November 5, 1968, Nixon won the election. When Nixon was inaugurated on January 20, 1969, he became the fifth U.S. president to deal with the Vietnam conflict.

Chicago police clubbed antiwar protesters at the Democratic National Convention in Chicago in August 1968. The United States seemed to be coming apart at the seams. "Chicago was a catastrophe," Democratic candidate Hubert H. Humphrey later said.

THE HOME FRONT

Protest!

The Vietnam War took place at a time of tremendous change in the United States. American society was struggling to address years and years of discrimination. Black Americans, women, and other minorities were standing up for equal rights. At the same time, young people were changing the face of American society and culture, as they threw over their parents' music, sexual morals, and styles. "Don't trust anyone over 30" was a popular expression on college campuses in the mid-1960s.

A student screams at a police officer after police used tear gas and clubs to break up an antiwar demonstration in Madison, Wisconsin, in the late 1960s.

This atmosphere of protest fed into, and was fed by, opposition to the war. Antiwar protests began in 1966. By 1967 they had become common. Respected public figures such as Martin Luther King Jr. and Senator J. William Fulbright (who had originally voted in favor of the Gulf of Tonkin Resolution) spoke out against the war. Many celebrities protested the war, including singer Joan Baez and actress Jane Fonda.

U.S. officials worried about the public's change of mind about American involvement in Vietnam. Yet they did not take significant steps to whip up sentiment in favor of war. According to Dean Rusk, secretary of state in the Johnson administration, "You didn't see members of the armed forces or units of the armed forces parading through American cities. You didn't see pretty movie stars out selling bonds in factories and things like that—all the things we did during World War II—because we felt that in this nuclear world, where thousands of megatons are lying around in the hands of frail human beings, it's just too dangerous for an entire people to become too angry."

Although the U.S. government did not spread much propaganda at home, it did take action against some war protesters. Government agents spied on some American groups that were believed to be run by Communists.

In one incident, aides to President Nixon broke into the office of a psychiatrist treating a former Defense Department analyst, Daniel Ellsberg. They were seeking material to embarrass Ellsberg, who had given the *New York Times* a copy of the Defense Department's secret internal history and analysis of the Vietnam War. The history, dubbed the "Pentagon Papers," showed that the Nixon and Johnson administrations had lied to the public about the war's progress. The Nixon administration fought publication of the Pentagon Papers in the courts. But the U.S. Supreme Court ruled against the government.

THE END BEGINS

Almost immediately after President Nixon took office, peace talks started again in Paris. But the negotiators made little progress. In Vietnam the fighting did not let up.

HAMBURGER HILL

On May 10, 1969, a bloody battle began in the A Shau Valley of South Vietnam. Communists used the valley as a route to the coastal area around Hue. To stop the Communists, U.S. troops were airlifted by helicopter into the valley. U.S. soldiers tried to take over one of the valley's hills, Dong Ap Bia, also called, simply, Hill 937. North Vietnamese soldiers held the hill for more than a week, raining fire down on Americans who tried to advance. Time after time, the U.S troops were ordered up the hill, only to be driven back by Communist

fire. Finally, on May 20, U.S. soldiers reached the top. Forty-six American soldiers died in the effort, and 400 were wounded.

Hill 937 became known as Hamburger Hill—*hamburger* because the fighting there chewed up so many men. "A lot of people felt it was [useless], of going up time and time again," said Patrick Power, who fought there. "There was a lot of anger over that. Everyone knew after the first company went up that we'd be walking into ambushes each and every time."

Yet the army ordered U.S. troops to abandon Hamburger Hill less than a month after they had taken it. The Americans left because they had accomplished their mission of driving North Vietnamese and Viet Cong troops from the area. As U.S. General Creighton Abrams explained, "We are not fighting for terrain as such. We are going after the enemy." After U.S. soldiers left, the North Vietnamese retook the hill without a fight. Many Americans were outraged at what they viewed as the needless loss of life.

According to Colonel Harry G. Summers, a Vietnam War veteran and historian, Hamburger Hill led President Nixon to end all major U.S. troop operations in the war. He wanted to keep future U.S. casualties to a minimum. This meant no more major search-and-destroy operations. Although the end of the war had not yet arrived, Hamburger Hill marked the beginning of the end.

War Dogs

Man's best friend has often been the soldier's best friend, too. Several thousand dogs served in specialized platoons in Vietnam. German shepherds worked as scout dogs. They silently patrolled ahead of troops on the lookout for snipers, ambushes, mines, and booby traps. Labrador retrievers served as trackers, picking up the enemy's trail when it had been lost. Other dogs patrolled the perimeters of army bases or sniffed out mines, traps, and tunnels.

A U.S. German shepherd assists its "fellow soldiers" on patrol.

These animals saved many lives. For example, Wolf, a German shepherd scout, stopped short while leading a platoon up a hill one day in 1970. Wolf's handler (human trainer) did not see anything out of the ordinary. He was about to step around the dog, but Wolf moved urgently to stop him. The dog even bit him on the hand. "And then I saw it," said Charlie Cargo, Wolf's handler and a member of the Army's Forty-eighth Scout Dog Platoon in Chu Lai. "A trip wire the thickness of a hair. Two feet in front of me." Had the platoon advanced any farther, they would have set off an explosive booby trap set by the Viet Cong.

Another soldier, Tom L. Farley, described a patrol in which a scout dog detected a trip wire, tracked down a Viet Cong camp, and searched the camp for booby traps and buried weapons. "During that one patrol," Farley wrote, "the dog had proved that he was, pound for pound, one of the most effective . . . weapons available to the American soldier." According to Vietnam veteran Steve Ball, war dogs prevented an estimated 10,000 American casualties in the war. Nearly 500 dogs were killed in action.

MEDICAL CARE

For every ten Americans who served in Vietnam, one became injured. Hidden land mines caused thousands to lose arms or legs. Other weapons, such as high-powered rifles, destroyed body tissue and organs. Low-tech booby traps could be equally deadly. Jeanne Rivera, a nurse and operating room supervisor in Vietnam in 1967 and 1968, remembered, "The wounds were always the dirtiest ones imaginable. Punji sticks, mud in the wounds, the material of their fatigues [uniforms] in the wounds, compound fractures. I mean big, big, big wounds."

In firefights in the field, medical corpsmen tended to the injured. There they applied bandages and gave pain medication. Medical evacuation helicopters—Medevacs—flew to battle scenes to airlift the wounded to hospitals. These airlifts became known as "dust-offs" because of the dust they kicked up during landing.

In field hospitals, doctors and nurses performed surgeries and other procedures. During periods of fighting, hospitals saw a constant stream of wounded men. "We got to a point where there was so much blood," Rivera remembered, "there was so much that I had holes put in the bottom of the operating room so we could clean the floor." Some wounded soldiers were taken to navy hospital ships stationed in the South China Sea.

Wounded American soliders often received medical care at or near combat sites.

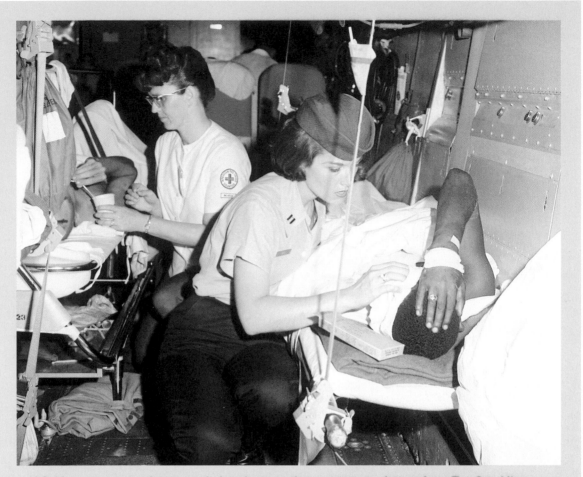

U.S. Navy nurses tend to wounded patients as they prepare to depart from Tan Son Nhut air base for the United States.

Injured soldiers called the nurses "Mom" and turned to them for comfort. Often, nurses would sit with dying soldiers, even if they were unconscious. "No one should die alone," said nurse Lorraine Boudreau, who served two tours in Vietnam.

Disease was a problem in Vietnam, although it killed far fewer troops than did combat injuries. Soldiers suffered from malaria and other illnesses caused by tropical parasites.

Injured North Vietnamese and Viet Cong received medical care from their own doctors and nurses. In the jungle, malaria and snakebites were major health hazards. The sick or wounded were often carried on bamboo stretchers for miles to the nearest Communist medical facility. Some hospitals were constructed underground to avoid detection.

VIETNAMIZATION

Upon taking office, President Nixon made a major change to U.S. war strategy: "Vietnamization." Vietnamization was the gradual shift of responsibility for fighting to the South Vietnamese. The idea was that Americans would train and equip the South Vietnamese. But the South Vietnamese would do the fighting. This was not a new idea. The first U.S. soldiers sent to Vietnam in the 1950s had been "military advisers." But the policy meant that U.S. soldiers would start coming home.

As the American approach to the war changed, the attitude of many troops changed, too. At first, they had been there to fight Communism and save the free world. But this did not seem to be the case any longer. Nineteen-year-old soldier Keith Franklin left a letter for his parents while visiting home in Salamanca, New

EYEWITNESS QUOTE:

"This war is so…frustrating and boring at times that it would try the pope's patience. It is made up of extended periods of boredom [mixed] with periods of utter mayhem [chaos]."

—Letter from Desmond Barry Jr., lieutenant, U.S. Marine Corps

York, in late 1969. The letter was to be opened in the event of his death.

"Dear Mom and Dad," Franklin wrote, "The war that has taken my life, and many thousands of others before me, is immoral, unlawful and an atrocity. . . . So, as I lie dead, please grant my last request. Help me to inform the American people. . . . Help me let them know that their silence is permitting this atrocity to go on and that my death will not be in vain if by prompting them to act I can in some way help to bring an end to the war that brought an end to my life." Franklin died in Cambodia in the spring of 1970.

"FRAGGING" AND BEYOND

Some American soldiers were so angry about the war that they turned against their own in a murderous practice known as "fragging." In fragging incidents, soldiers

Death of Ho Chi Minh

On September 3, 1969, Ho Chi Minh died of a heart attack at the age of seventy-nine. He had been in ill health for years. His successor was Vietnamese Communist Party chief Le Duan. In his will, Ho urged the North Vietnamese to fight "until the last Yankee [American] has gone."

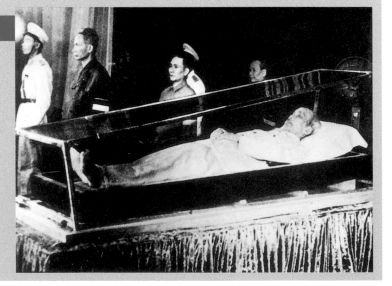

attacked and killed their superiors and even fellow soldiers with fragmentation grenades and other weapons. Many U.S. soldiers tried to escape the boredom and horror of the war by taking illegal drugs. According to Karen Bush, a nurse in Pleiku in 1969 and 1970, "You could get drugs anywhere. You could buy them on the open market. . . . Peer pressure over there [to take drugs] was very, very high."

Citizens in the United States shared the soldiers' frustrations. Antiwar protests continued across America, even though large numbers of troops were being withdrawn under President Nixon's Vietnamization policy. The protesters were noisy, sometimes violent, and mostly young. They did not trust those in authority, and they did not hesitate to oppose U.S. policy.

President Nixon, his advisers, and many Americans believed that the protesters who criticized the war were aiding the Communists. On November 3, 1969, President Nixon made a speech to the nation on national television. In it he asked for support from "the great silent majority of my fellow Americans." Nixon believed that most Americans—the "silent majority"—did not share the antiwar protesters' beliefs. The president urged, "Let us be united for peace. Let us also be united against defeat. Because let us understand: North Vietnam cannot defeat or humiliate the United States. Only Americans can do that."

Nixon's speech was widely quoted. Yet less than two weeks later, some 250,000 people gathered in Washington, D.C., for the largest antiwar protest in U.S. history.

Hundreds of thousands of antiwar protesters gathered in Washington, D.C., on November 15, 1969.

A NEW DECADE: CAMBODIA

Vietnamization did not mean that the United States was abandoning South Vietnam. U.S. leaders were concerned about North Vietnamese and Viet Cong sanctuaries (safe hiding places) in Cambodia, Vietnam's neighbor. Cambodia was neutral—it had not taken sides in the war. Yet for years, the North Vietnamese and Viet Cong violated this neutrality. They used Cambodia as a place to prepare for attacks in South Vietnam. Viet Cong forces also hid there after attacks.

In 1969 President Nixon ordered the bombing of Communist sanctuaries in Cambodia. This decision was kept a secret from the American public. In the spring of 1970, President Nixon and his advisers

U.S. air strikes pummeled Viet Cong bases in Cambodia in May 1970. The Cambodian raid sparked new antiwar protests in the United States.

decided that more needed to be done against the Viet Cong in Cambodia.

On April 30, 1970, the president made an announcement on national television. "Tonight, American and South Vietnamese units will attack the headquarters for the entire Communist military operation in South Vietnam," he said. "This key control center has been occupied by the North Vietnamese and Viet Cong for five years in blatant violation of Cambodia's neutrality. This is not an invasion of Cambodia."

American and South Vietnamese soldiers captured or destroyed huge supplies of food, weapons, and ammunition hidden by the Communists in Cambodia. The incursion, or raid, lasted two months.

FAST FACT

RHYMES WITH "MARVIN"
Americans called their allies in the South Vietnamese Army "ARVN"—for Army of Vietnam. They pronounced the term "AHR-vihn."

KENT STATE

The Cambodia incursion created more protest in the United States. In May 1970, demonstrations broke out at hundreds of colleges and universities. A demonstration at Kent State University in Ohio horrified the nation and shocked the world.

On May 4, hundreds of students had gathered to protest at Kent State. Ohio governor James Rhodes called out the Ohio National Guard to keep the situation under control. The protesters set fire to a building.

They threw stones at the soldiers. In the midst of the confusion, the guardsmen fired into the crowd. Four students were shot dead. Eleven others were wounded.

The sight of Americans killing Americans stunned the nation. Colleges and universities closed down. Nearly 100,000 protesters gathered outside the White House and other buildings in Washington, D.C. Even as U.S. soldiers were coming home, the war was still tearing at the fabric of American society.

The shootings at Kent State University on May 4, 1970, were front-page news around the world. This photograph of a young woman kneeling over one of the dead protesters became a symbol of the war.

7 AMERICA LETS GO

By the spring of 1972, fewer than 100,000 U.S. soldiers were in Vietnam. The American public remained divided over the war. The year before, the South Vietnamese had done poorly in their first major test of fighting on their own. The North Vietnamese took advantage of this weakness to launch a dramatic strike.

In March 1972, the Communists began the biggest offensive of the war. Called the Easter Offensive, the attack involved more than 200,000 North Vietnamese regular troops. The soldiers moved against cities and bases throughout South Vietnam. "I never dreamed anything like that was possible, to put so many rounds [of ammunition] in one small area in such a short period of time," said U.S. Army Captain Harold Moffett Jr., who came under attack at An Loc, sixty miles from Saigon.

The Easter Offensive continued through the spring, summer, and fall of 1972. The North Vietnamese were pushing for the total conquest of South Vietnam, and their goal seemed within reach. The United States either had to act or watch as South Vietnam collapsed.

President Nixon authorized a major bombing campaign against North Vietnam. The president also ordered the mining of North Vietnam's Haiphong Harbor. U.S. Navy aircraft dropped devices in the harbor that would explode if ships sailed past them. This interfered with North Vietnam's ability to receive war supplies. For the time being, the takeover of South Vietnam was halted.

THE VIET CONG AND THE NORTH VIETNAMESE POINT OF VIEW

The Viet Cong and the North Vietnamese were fighting the war for many different reasons. Some South Vietnamese joined or supported the Viet Cong to free their country from foreign influence. Doan Van Toai was vice president of the Saigon Student Union in 1969 and 1970. "I learned the history of my country's thousand-year struggle against Chinese occupation and its century-long effort against Western domination," he explained. "With this background my [friends] and I grew up with a hatred of foreign intervention."

Many South Vietnamese helped the Viet Cong, but not all of them were motivated by ideas about nationalism or politics. They wanted to be able to feed their families and live in peace. Some believed that the Viet Cong would make that possible. Others believed that the Viet Cong would kill them if they did not cooperate—so they cooperated.

The North Vietnamese Communists wanted to unify the people and nation of Vietnam, north and south. They also wanted to have a unified government for all of Vietnam, and they wanted it to be their government—which was Communist.

The Communists wanted their party to rule a unified Vietnam. They also sought to prevent those who disagreed with their Communist system from gaining influence or power.

Children in Hanoi hold a poster of Ho Chi Minh.

PEACE ON A PENDULUM

Meanwhile, U.S. combat troops continued to leave Vietnam. U.S. policymakers realized that South Vietnam was going to have a difficult time defending itself alone. So Nixon's staff looked for diplomatic ways to end the war. The Paris peace talks had been an off-and-on affair ever since they had begun in 1968. Yet President Nixon's special assistant for national security affairs, Henry Kissinger, had often met secretly with North Vietnamese officials.

The United States took other steps that put pressure on the North Vietnamese to negotiate. In February 1972, President Nixon made an historic visit to China. There he met with that nation's Communist leaders, Mao Zedong and Zhou Enlai. In May Nixon visited the Soviet Union, meeting with the Communist chief there, Leonid Brezhnev. These trips were a sign of better relations between the United States and its longtime opponents. The visits worried Le Duan and other North Vietnamese leaders. They needed the support of China and the Soviet Union. This concern helped convince the North Vietnamese to meet again for peace talks in Paris in the summer of 1972.

President Nixon was eager for peace. He faced an election in November 1972. His opponent for the presidency was Democratic senator George McGovern. McGovern had said that he would immediately withdraw troops from Vietnam if elected.

A month before the election, Henry Kissinger and North Vietnamese negotiator Le Duc Tho reached a peace accord. As part of the agreement, the United States dropped its demand that North Vietnam's troops leave the south. The North Vietnamese dropped their position that South Vietnamese president Thieu had to be removed from the government.

In Saigon President Thieu was angered by the deal. He did not want tens of thousands of North Vietnamese troops in South Vietnam. Nonetheless, Kissinger announced to the press on October 26, 1972, "We believe that peace is at hand. We believe that an agreement is in sight."

Just two weeks later, President Nixon won a landslide victory over Democrat George McGovern in the presidential election. Nixon won in every state except Massachusetts. The vote showed that most Americans preferred Nixon's promised "peace with honor" to McGovern's "immediate and complete withdrawal." But despite Henry Kissinger's announcement that peace was at hand, the war continued.

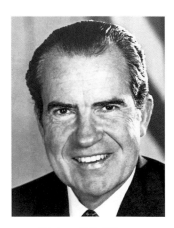

Richard M. Nixon

CHRISTMAS BOMBING

On December 13, 1972, the Paris peace talks fell apart again when the United States, at the request of President Thieu, asked for changes in the Kissinger-Le Duc Tho agreement. But the North Vietnamese would not compromise. President Nixon made an important decision: he would try to force North Vietnam to change its mind with another bombing campaign.

The Christmas bombing campaign, as it was called, was the largest of the entire war. In a two-week period, B-52 bombers flew more than 3,000 missions and dropped 40,000 tons of bombs on the northern cities of Hanoi and Haiphong. Many American and international leaders spoke out against the Christmas bombing. Yet the campaign was successful. On December 30, 1972, President Nixon announced that the North Vietnamese had agreed to continue discussions. The bombing campaign was halted.

PARIS PEACE ACCORDS

This time, U.S. leaders were determined to end the war. The United States went along with North Vietnam's demand that its troops remain in the south. President Thieu objected, but the U.S. government gave him no choice. If South Vietnam wanted to continue to receive U.S. aid, it had to agree. On January 27, 1973, representatives of the United States, North Vietnam, South Vietnam, and the Viet Cong's Provisional Revolutionary Government signed the Paris Peace Accords.

Under the agreement, North Vietnam agreed to stop fighting against the south immediately. It also promised to release all U.S. prisoners of war (POWs) within sixty days. The United States agreed to halt all military action in Vietnam and to remove the rest of its

U.S. negotiator William H. Sullivan *(lower right)* and North Vietnamese negotiator Xuan Thuy *(upper right)* watch as Henry Kissinger *(lower center)* and Le Duc Tho *(second from upper right)* sign the Paris Peace Accords.

soldiers. North Vietnamese troops were allowed to remain in South Vietnam. South Vietnam was considered one country with two governments—one led by President Thieu, the other by the Provisional Revolutionary Government. As for the future, the accords stated: "The reunification of Vietnam shall be carried out step by step through peaceful means . . . without coercion [force]."

BITTERNESS AND PROMISES

By April 1, 1973, only a handful of Americans remained in South Vietnam. North Vietnam released 591 U.S. POWs by the deadline as well.

Leaders of South Vietnam's government were bitter about the cease-fire. But President Thieu could take heart from one gesture extended by the United States. "You have my absolute assurance," President Nixon wrote in a letter to Thieu, "that if Hanoi fails to abide by the terms of this agreement, it is my intention to take swift and severe retaliatory action." In other words, Nixon was promising to defend South Vietnam from North Vietnam. In addition, because the cease-fire applied only to Vietnamese territory, the United States continued to bomb the Ho Chi Minh Trail in Cambodia.

But President Nixon would be unable to keep his promise. In November Congress

This U.S. Air Force photo shows a trail of damaged and destroyed trucks on the Ho Chi Minh Trail.

passed the War Powers Act, which limited the president's power to send U.S. troops abroad without congressional approval. This made further U.S. military involvement in Southeast Asia—including bombing the Ho Chi Minh Trail—impossible.

WATERGATE SCANDAL

The political scandal known as Watergate dealt another blow to President Nixon's promise to come to Thieu's aid. Back in 1972, when Nixon was running for reelection, some of his supporters were involved in a burglary of the Democratic campaign headquarters in the Watergate office buildings in Washington, D.C. After the break-in, top Nixon aides tried to cover it up. But newspaper reporters investigated the affair. They discovered that Nixon's staff had committed many illegal acts. As more information became public, top Nixon aides resigned. Vice President Spiro T. Agnew resigned in connection with yet another political scandal. He was replaced by Congressman Gerald Ford, minority leader of the House of Representatives.

Congress held televised hearings on Watergate in the spring and summer of 1974. Details of the Nixon administration's so-called "dirty tricks" were revealed and examined. The president himself was accused of political and possibly criminal wrongdoing. The House of Representatives was ready to impeach Nixon. According to the U.S. Constitution, Nixon would then be required to stand trial in the Senate.

Disgraced and weary from fighting the Watergate scandal, Richard Nixon resigned as president on August 9, 1974. Vice

THE WHITE HOUSE
WASHINGTON

August 9, 1974

Dear Mr. Secretary:

I hereby resign the Office of President of the United States.

Sincerely,

Richard Nixon

11.35 AM

HK

The Honorable Henry A. Kissinger
The Secretary of State
Washington, D. C. 20520

Nixon's letter of resignation is addressed to Henry Kissinger, secretary of state.

President Gerald Ford became the thirty-eighth president of the United States.

NORTHERN ASSAULT

In Vietnam the 1973 peace agreement was unraveling. Thousands died in fighting between Communists and South Vietnamese in the countryside. In December 1974, North Vietnam attacked a South Vietnamese province. This was a clear violation of the peace accords. But President Gerald Ford could not send in U.S. bombers or soldiers. His hands were tied by the War Powers Act. Former President Nixon's promise to respond to Communist attacks could not be kept.

Without the U.S. standing in their way, the North Vietnamese launched a major

invasion. In early March 1975, North Vietnamese troops pushed into the central highlands. The city of Ban Me Thuot fell within a day. President Thieu decided to evacuate South Vietnamese forces from the highlands and northern provinces. He felt his best chance to hold onto the country would be to concentrate his forces in the coastal cities.

The sudden decision to retreat set off a massive and disorganized evacuation of civilians and soldiers. Thousands packed their belongings in cars or trucks, on bicycles, or on their backs. A column of people and vehicles twenty miles long wound its way toward the coast.

As the North Vietnamese advanced toward Saigon, South Vietnam was coming apart. South Vietnamese soldiers fled toward the coast, leaving millions of dollars' worth of U.S. military equipment behind. Hue fell to the Communists, with little resistance. Da Nang fell next, on March 30, 1975.

Only Saigon remained in the hands of the Thieu government. With the North Vietnamese ready to take over the country, the U.S. government and private relief (aid) groups organized Operation Babylift. This operation evacuated thousands of Vietnamese infants and young children and took them to safety in other countries. But

Thousands of Vietnamese refugees fled before the North Vietnamese advance in 1975. Without American air support, the South Vietnamese army crumbled.

the first evacuation flight—a huge C-5A transport carrying more than 200 orphans plus American escorts—crashed shortly after takeoff. Many of the passengers died. "Never mind, we have plenty more to send you," a Vietnamese military officer bitterly told reporter Malcolm Browne.

Figures vary, but Operation Babylift brought about 2,000 orphans to the United States. About 1,300 were sent to Canada, Europe, and Australia—very few of the total number of children orphaned by the war.

"WHITE CHRISTMAS"

As North Vietnamese troops bore down on Saigon on April 21, President Thieu resigned and flew to Taiwan. In a televised speech, he blamed the United States for South Vietnam's defeat. "The United States has not respected its promises," Thieu said. "It is inhumane. It is untrustworthy. It is irresponsible."

Before dawn on Tuesday, April 29, 1975, North Vietnamese forces started attacking the Tan Son Nhut air base in Saigon. With South Vietnamese civilians and soldiers frantic to leave their country, President Ford authorized Operation Frequent Wind. This was a helicopter evacuation of the remaining Americans in Saigon. It also included as many South Vietnamese as possible. When a radio station in Saigon broadcast the song "White Christmas," a prearranged signal, Americans knew the time for evacuation had come.

Evacuation sites in downtown Saigon became mob scenes. An overwhelming number of South Vietnamese wanted to

Saigon residents made a mad rush to escape the Communist invasion. U.S. and South Vietnamese helicopters airlifted many to ships stationed off the Vietnamese coast.

escape before the North Vietnamese took over. U.S. Marines tried to keep order over the desperate crowds. Knowing they themselves couldn't escape, parents pushed their small children into the arms of fleeing Americans. Helicopters airlifted 1,000 Americans and 6,000 South Vietnamese to a fleet of waiting ships offshore. Because there was no room on the ships for the aircraft, many pilots ditched their helicopters in the sea after delivering their human cargo. Boats then plucked the pilots out of the water.

Tens of thousands of South Vietnamese managed to escape by boat. Some took to the sea in their own small craft, including rafts. U.S. merchant and military ships took on many of these desperate refugees. Others arranged rides on planes that landed in Thailand and other destinations.

On the morning of April 30, General Duong Van Minh announced South Vietnam's surrender. (Minh, one of the generals who had overthrown President Diem a dozen years earlier, had taken over the presidency when Thieu fled.) As hundreds of pro-Communist South Vietnamese cheered, North Vietnamese and Viet Cong troops rode through the streets of Saigon in trucks, tanks, and armored vehicles. They raised the flag of the National Liberation Front over the presidential palace. The war was over.

North Vietnamese tanks roll through Saigon in 1975, ending the war. Saigon would later be renamed Ho Chi Minh City.

EPILOGUE

The victorious Communists did not have a forgive-and-forget attitude toward the defeated South Vietnamese. They forced hundreds of thousands into "reeducation camps"—that is, prisons. For many, imprisonment lasted years. Many died in prison, and others were executed. In 1976 the northern and southern parts of Vietnam were officially merged into one country, the Socialist Republic of Vietnam. Saigon was renamed Ho Chi Minh City.

Some former Viet Cong quickly became disappointed with the North Vietnamese Communists. Truong Nhu Tang, minister of justice in the Provisional Revolutionary Government, said, "With total power in their hands, they began to show their cards in the most brutal fashion. They made it understood that the Vietnam of the future . . . would be ground and molded by the political machine of the conquerors." Tang retired from the government in 1976. He eventually fled the country.

Doan Van Toai had resisted the Thieu government as a student. He later worked for the Provisional Revolutionary Government. Toai also came to reject the Communist regime. Toai was disgusted by the new leaders' commitment to work "under the leadership of the Soviet Union." He also found that "the [new] Vietnamese rulers have arrested hundreds of thousands of individuals—not only those who had cooperated with the Thieu regime but even those who had not, including religious leaders and former members of the N.L.F." Toai left Vietnam in 1978.

Hundreds of thousands of people fled the harsh rule the victorious North Vietnamese Communists set up after the 1975 takeover. Many set out for the South China Sea in small boats, headed for Thailand or Malaysia. Their vessels were not built for a long voyage. Some people were rescued. Many died at sea or at the hands of pirates.

LEGACIES

The Vietnam War divided Americans while Americans were fighting it. It continued to divide them after the Americans came home. Some believed the war was a product of the arrogant belief by U.S. leaders that they had a right to control a small country across the globe.

Others felt that the United States was entitled to take military action in another nation to stop the spread of Communism. Yet some of these same people felt that the domino theory did not apply to Vietnam. They did not think important U.S. interests were at stake if Vietnam became a Communist nation. Still others felt that the domino theory was correct and that the American involvement in Vietnam was an important reason Communism did not spread to all the countries in Southeast Asia, such as Indonesia, the Philippines, Malaysia, Singapore, and Thailand.

To some, the United States was guilty of a shameful betrayal of the South Vietnamese. They felt that, having made the

The Boat People

In 1979 a new wave of refugees took to the sea in small boats. Many of these were Vietnamese people of Chinese ethnicity. In a complex turn of events, China and Vietnam fought a short but bitter war in 1979. Vietnam had invaded Cambodia, which had come under the rule of a brutal dictator named Pol Pot. China supported Pol Pot and invaded Vietnam to pressure Vietnam to withdraw from Cambodia. As a result of this fighting, the Vietnamese government forced nearly half a million Chinese to leave Vietnam. These and other refugees from Vietnam became known as "boat people."

Hundreds of thousands of Vietnamese risked starvation and drowning to leave Vietnam by boat.

commitment to mold a non-Communist South Vietnam, Americans should not have deserted the country.

There is no single truth about the war. The arguments about Vietnam have never been truly settled. They probably never will be.

But one conclusion is sure: the war produced deep changes in American society. After Vietnam, U.S. leaders have looked for the approval of the American people before sending troops overseas. Americans also became more skeptical about their political leaders. They are more likely to question those in power. This skepticism probably helped fuel the women's rights and environmental movements in the United States.

Other changes came about too. As a result of Vietnam, Congress lowered the voting age from twenty-one to eighteen in 1970. This change was based on the theory that young people who were old enough to fight were also old enough to vote. This change became the Twenty-sixth Amendment to the U.S. Constitution in 1971. President Nixon ended the draft, which had caused so much controversy throughout the war, in 1973. Since then, the U.S. military has relied on volunteers.

HEALING THE WOUNDS

Americans and Vietnamese took steps to heal the wounds caused by the war. Presidents Gerald Ford and Jimmy Carter created programs to forgive those who had violated the draft laws. In 1989 the Vietnamese government agreed to take back thousands of refugees who had fled following the war and not to punish them.

Amerasian Children

Among the victims of the war were thousands of children born to Vietnamese women and fathered by American soldiers. Many of these Amerasian children were left behind when their American fathers left for home. Some were abandoned when the United States pulled out of Vietnam in 1975. Because of their mixed heritage, the children became outcasts in Vietnamese society at the end of the war. Although welfare programs and children's groups tried to help the Amerasians, many turned to begging and lived on the streets.

Vietnam continued its Communist form of government, but its Communist sponsor, the Soviet Union, broke apart in 1991.

For many Americans, a major obstacle kept them from healing the social and psychological wounds of war. This was the uncertainty surrounding more than 2,000 Americans who were missing in action (MIA) when the United States pulled out of Vietnam in 1975. It was unknown whether these soldiers had been killed or were perhaps still imprisoned. In 1992 the Vietnamese government agreed to allow U.S. Department of Defense employees to search for MIAs in Vietnam. In 1993 the remains of sixty-seven Americans were brought home to the United States. The search to find missing Americans—or at least to determine where and how they died and to recover their remains—continues to this day.

Vietnamese cooperation on the MIA issue helped lead to the renewal of friendly relations between the United

Volunteers work at the grim task of digging for the remains of American MIAs.

States and Vietnam in 1995. President Bill Clinton appointed Douglas "Pete" Peterson as ambassador to a new U.S. embassy in Hanoi. Peterson had been a navy pilot during the war. He spent more than six years as a POW in Hanoi, not far from the new embassy.

The action that may have produced the greatest healing was the building of the Vietnam Veterans Memorial in Washington, D.C. The memorial was the idea of Vietnam veteran Jan Scruggs. He wanted to honor each American who had died in Vietnam. "All their names will be there," he told his wife of his vision in 1979. With help from two other Vietnam veterans, Scruggs created an organization to raise money to build the memorial. Congress agreed to provide public land in Washington, D.C., for the memorial.

To choose a designer for the Vietnam Veterans Memorial, Scruggs's organization held a competition. More than 1,400 individuals and teams submitted designs. The competition judges unanimously chose the entry of twenty-one-year-old Maya Lin, a student at Yale University. Lin's design was a V-shaped wall of black granite, polished to a gloss and inscribed with the names of all the Americans who had died in the war.

On November 11, 1982—Veterans Day —150,000 Vietnam veterans and others gathered for the formal dedication of the memorial. The memorial recognized those

The Vietnam Veterans Memorial was dedicated on November 11, 1982. The memorial has helped to heal the wounds of a nation divided by war.

who had made the ultimate sacrifice for their country. It also recognized the service of the Americans who had survived the war in a separate statue called The Three Servicemen. Many soldiers who survived the unpopular war had been criticized when they came home from fighting in Vietnam. The statue demonstrated that their service to their country was finally recognized. The Vietnam Veterans Memorial, often called simply "the Wall," became one of the most visited sites in the nation's capital. Drawn to its sad beauty, visitors study the 58,226 names of those who died. Many leave letters, poems, photographs, stuffed animals, and other gifts in honor of the dead. In 1993 the Vietnam Women's Memorial was dedicated nearby, honoring nurses and other women who served in the war.

And so this memorial to the conflict that so bitterly divided Americans brings them together—not to relive the horrors and divisiveness, but to remember the soldiers who died doing what their country asked them to do, so far from home.

SELECTED EVENTS OF THE VIETNAM WAR

Because the war had no front lines and few major battles, a complete listing of its events cannot be clearly shown on a single map. Please see other maps in this book for additional details.

Siege of Dien Bien Phu **(French versus Viet Minh forces)**	**March–May 1954**
Gulf of Tonkin Incident	**August 2–4, 1964**
U.S. air raids	**1965–1973**
Pleiku	**February 7, 1965**
Ia Drang	**November 14–20, 1965**
Operation Cedar Falls	**January 1967**
Operation Junction City	**February–May 1967**
Siege of Khe Sanh	**January–April 1968**
A Shau Valley/Hamburger Hill	**May 1969**
Cambodian Incursion	**April–May 1970**
Easter Offensive	**April–July 1972**
Mining of Haiphong Harbor	**May 1972**
Surrender of Saigon	**April 30, 1975**

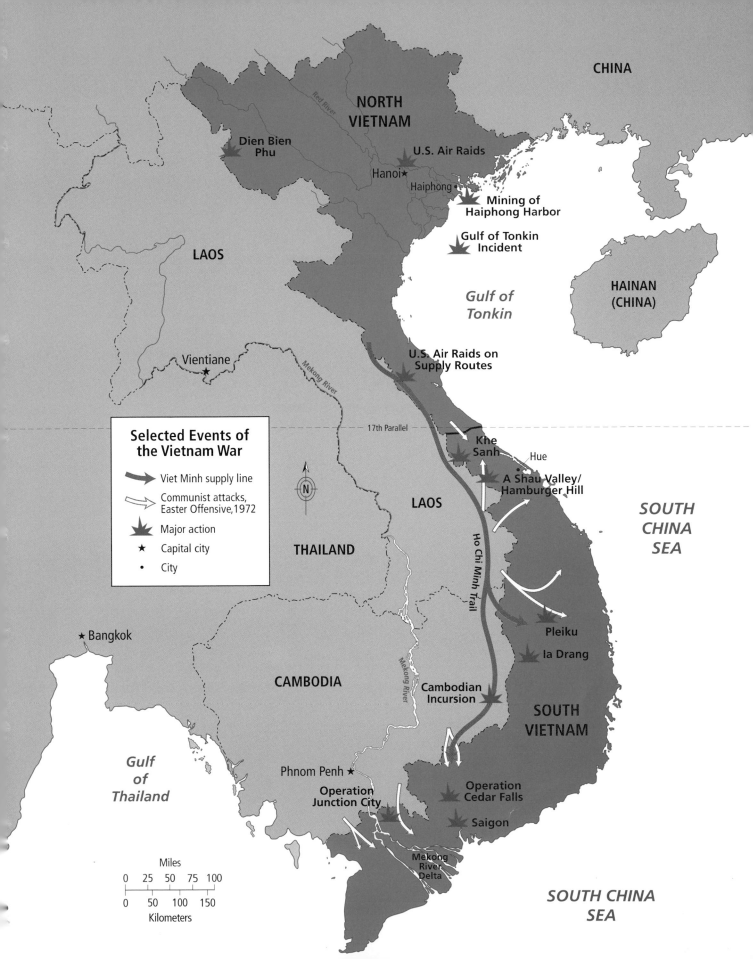

CHINA

NORTH VIETNAM

Dien Bien Phu

U.S. Air Raids

Hanoi ★

Haiphong

Mining of Haiphong Harbor

Gulf of Tonkin Incident

LAOS

Red River

Gulf of Tonkin

HAINAN (CHINA)

Vientiane ★

Mekong River

U.S. Air Raids on Supply Routes

17th Parallel

Khe Sanh

Hue

A Shau Valley/ Hamburger Hill

SOUTH CHINA SEA

Selected Events of the Vietnam War

➜ Viet Minh supply line

⇨ Communist attacks, Easter Offensive,1972

✶ Major action

★ Capital city

• City

N

THAILAND

LAOS

Ho Chi Minh Trail

Pleiku

Ia Drang

Bangkok ★

CAMBODIA

Mekong River

Cambodian Incursion

SOUTH VIETNAM

Gulf of Thailand

Phnom Penh ★

Operation Junction City

Operation Cedar Falls

Saigon

Mekong River Delta

SOUTH CHINA SEA

Miles
0   25   50   75 100

Kilometers
0   50   100   150

VIETNAM WAR TIMELINE

1941   Ho Chi Minh and others form the Viet Minh to fight the Japanese and French occupation of Vietnam.

1945   World War II ends. Ho Chi Minh announces the creation of the Democratic Republic of Vietnam.

1946   The first Vietnam war begins between the Viet Minh and France.

1954   Viet Minh troops defeat French forces at Dien Bien Phu on May 7.
In July the Geneva Agreement temporarily divides Vietnam in two parts, with Ho Chi Minh's government taking control of the north and Bao Dai's government ruling the south.

1955   The United States begins military and economic aid and military training for Bao Dai's government. In October Ngo Dinh Diem takes over from Bao Dai after an election and forms the Republic of Vietnam in the south.

1958   The National Liberation Front and Viet Cong become active in South Vietnam, calling for the overthrow of Diem's government and carrying out acts of violence against Diem loyalists.

1963   A group of South Vietnamese generals overthrows President Diem on November 1. Diem is killed in the coup.

1964   Reports of North Vietnamese attacks on a U.S. ship in the Gulf of Tonkin prompt President Lyndon Johnson to respond by bombing targets in North Vietnam.

1965   A group of 3,500 U.S. marines lands at Da Nang in March.
President Johnson authorizes Operation Rolling Thunder, the ongoing bombing of North Vietnam and the Ho Chi Minh Trail in March.

1966   U.S. forces begin large search-and-destroy operations against the Viet Cong and North Vietnamese forces in South Vietnam.

1967   Prominent Americans, including Martin Luther King Jr. and Senator Robert F. Kennedy, oppose the U.S. role in Vietnam.

1968   North Vietnamese and Viet Cong troops launch an attack on the U.S. air base at Khe Sanh in January. This is followed by the Tet Offensive, a widespread surprise attack throughout South Vietnam. In May, peace talks begin, but quickly collapse.

1969   President Richard Nixon begins withdrawing U.S. troops from Vietnam as part of his policy of "Vietnamization."

1970   U.S. and South Vietnamese troops cross the border into Cambodia to try to destroy North Vietnamese and Viet Cong sanctuaries in the Cambodian jungle.

1972   North Vietnamese and Viet Cong troops launch the Easter Offensive throughout South Vietnam in March.

1973   On January 27, the Paris Peace Accords are signed. U.S. troops are out of Vietnam by April 1.

1975   North Vietnam invades South Vietnam. On April 30, South Vietnam surrenders to North Vietnam.

GLOSSARY

Buddhist: a follower of one of the many types of Buddhism, a religion based on the teachings of Siddhartha Gautama, known as The Buddha, a sixth-century B.C. philosopher

capitalism: an economic system in which private companies and individuals, rather than the state (government), own and control factories, farms, business firms, and other means of production

colonialism: the conquest or control of one nation by another. Often, the ruling nation creates settlements of its own citizens in the colonized nation.

Communism: a governmental and economic system in which a single political party is in power and the state controls the economy. Such government economic control includes state ownership of most businesses. Usually, the party and state are all-powerful. They control most aspects of society.

coup: a sudden overthrow. Often used to describe the overthrow of a government.

democracy: a system of government in which citizens govern themselves, often by some type of majority rule. Democratic governments are generally representative democracies. This means voters elect representatives who govern for them.

domino theory: an American foreign policy that was based on the fear that a Communist takeover of one Southeast Asian nation would lead to more Communist takeovers in the region, one on top of the other, like dominoes.

guerrilla warfare: fighting that often features surprise attacks and quick retreats

infantry: troops that fight on land

MIA: missing in action; lost (usually in combat) and never found

military advisers: American troops sent to South Vietnam to train and assist the South Vietnamese military

sanctuaries: safe areas. Viet Cong sanctuaries were often hidden in jungles or outside the territory of South Vietnam, in Cambodia and Laos.

siege: a military blockade created to force a base or fort to surrender

WHO'S WHO?

Ho Chi Minh (1890–1969)

Born in central Vietnam in 1890, Ho left as a young man to travel the world. He returned to Vietnam in 1941 and founded the Viet Minh. He led the Viet Minh in their fight against the Japanese occupiers and Vichy French and became president of the new country he proclaimed in 1945—the Democratic Republic of Vietnam, or North Vietnam. Ho remained president of North Vietnam during much of the war against the south and the United States. He died in September 1969.

Henry Kissinger (b. 1923)

As President Richard Nixon's special assistant for national security affairs, Kissinger negotiated an end to the Vietnam War with North Vietnam's Le Duc Tho. The two men met for formal peace talks in Paris but also met secretly when official negotiations broke down. Kissinger and Le Duc Tho were awarded the Nobel Peace Prize in 1973 for their work in achieving a settlement of the Vietnam War. In 1973 President Nixon appointed the German-born Kissinger secretary of state, a position he continued to hold under President Gerald Ford.

Le Duan (1908–1986)

Like many Indochinese revolutionaries, Le fled Vietnam as a young man. He was arrested by the French when he returned in 1930. Upon his release from jail, Le Duan worked with Ho Chi Minh and the Viet Minh to overthrow the French. Le Duan became Ho Chi Minh's second in command in 1960. After Ho's death in 1969, Le Duan took his place as the leader of Vietnam. Le Duan died in 1986.

Robert McNamara (b. 1916)

McNamara became President John F. Kennedy's secretary of defense in 1961. He stayed in the position when Lyndon Johnson became president. McNamara was one of the chief architects of the Vietnam War. He supported the "domino theory." By 1967, however, he had come to believe that the United States could not win the war. After this time, he called for a smaller American presence in Vietnam. Unable to convince President Johnson of his new point of view, McNamara left the administration in 1968.

Ngo Dinh Diem (1901–1963)

Diem was born into a Catholic family with close ties to the French colonial government. He studied at a French school in Vietnam and went on to work in the French colonial government. Diem did favor Vietnam's independence from France, however. He left Vietnam in 1950. Diem returned to Vietnam in 1954, when Bao Dai asked him to become prime minister of the new South Vietnam. Diem soon ousted Bao Dai to become Vietnam's president and sole head of state. Diem enjoyed strong American support at first. But his brutal rule caused that support to crumble. In 1963 a group of South Vietnamese generals overthrew Diem in a coup, in which he was murdered.

Madame Ngo Dinh Nhu (b. 1924)

The wife of Ngo Dinh Nhu, President Diem's younger brother, she and her husband both served as political advisers to the president. Because Diem was unmarried, Madame Nhu served as the first lady of South Vietnam. Widely criticized as the "Dragon Lady," she alienated many people with her insensitive remarks about Buddhists and her arrogant manner. Madame Nhu survived the 1963 coup, in which her husband and President Diem were killed, by fleeing the country.

Nguyen Van Thieu (1923–2001)

Briefly a member of the Viet Minh, he rejected that group's Communist principles and joined the French-created Vietnamese army. In 1965 he and Nguyen Cao Ky came to power in South Vietnam. By 1967 Thieu was president. At first, Thieu seemed to bring some stability to South Vietnam. But Thieu's harsh actions spurred many South Vietnamese to oppose him. Thieu fled South Vietnam just before the Communists marched into Saigon in April 1975. He lived in Taiwan and Great Britain before immigrating to the United States, where he died in Boston in 2001.

Eleanor Ardel Vietti (1927–?)

As a doctor working at a jungle clinic in South Vietnam, she became the first female American prisoner of war. Dr. Vietti volunteered to care for Montagnards—tribal Vietnamese mountain people—who contracted leprosy at rates far higher than the general population. Christian missionary groups unrelated to the U.S. military sponsored the clinic where she worked. On May 30, 1962, a group of armed Viet Cong kidnapped Vietti and two others. Their fate remains unknown.

Vo Nguyen Giap (b. 1911)

As a college student in Hue, he joined the anti-French movement in the 1920s and later became one of the founders of the Viet Minh. He became defense minister in Ho Chi Minh's government in 1945 and led Viet Minh troops to their victory over France in 1954. Giap went on to serve as the top North Vietnamese general in the war against the south and the United States. After the war, he remained defense minister until 1980, after which he headed a science and technology commission. In 1992 Giap was awarded North Vietnam's highest honor, the Gold Star Order.

William Westmoreland (b. 1914)

Westmoreland was an Eagle Scout, high school class president, and award-winning cadet at West Point (the U.S. Military Academy). He commanded an artillery battalion in World War II. He went on to serve as commander of the army's 101st Airborne Division and superintendent of the U.S. Military Academy. In 1964 President Lyndon Johnson selected Westmoreland to command U.S. forces in Vietnam. General Westmoreland repeatedly argued that more American soldiers were necessary to win the war. After the Tet Offensive in 1968, President Johnson replaced Westmoreland with General Creighton Abrams.

SOURCE NOTES

4 Ho Chi Minh, "Declaration of Independence, Democratic Republic of Vietnam," *The Australian National University Home Page,* n.d., <http://www.coombs.anu.edu.au/~vern/van_kien/declar.html> (May 23, 2003).

4 Truong Nhu Tang, *A Viet Cong Memoir: An Inside Account of the Vietnam War and Its Aftermath* (New York: Vintage Books, 1985), 6.

4 PBS Online, "Transcript—Roots of a War," *The American Experience: Vietnam Online,* 1997, <http://www.pbs.org/wgbh/amex/vietnam/101ts.html> (May 23, 2003).

11 Stanley Karnow, *Vietnam: A History* (New York: Penguin Books, 1991), 163.

13 The History Place, "The Vietnam War: Seeds of Conflict, 1945–1960," *Historyplace.com,* n.d., <http://www.historyplace.com/unitedstates/vietnam/index-1945.html> (May 23, 2003).

14 Karnow, *Vietnam,* 192–193.

16 Robert S. McNamara, *In Retrospect: The Tragedy and Lessons of Vietnam* (New York: Times Books, 1995), 31.

16 CNN Interactive, "Interview: Vo Nguyen Giap," *The Cold War: Vietnam,* n.d., <http://www.cnn.com/SPECIALS/cold.war/episodes/11/interviews/giap> (May 23, 2003).

19 The History Place, "The Vietnam War: Seeds of Conflict, 1945–1960," *Historyplace.com.*

20 Gene Gurney, *Vietnam: The War in the Air* (New York: Crown Publishers, 1985), 10.

20 John F. Kennedy, "Inaugural Address, January 20, 1961," *John Fitzgerald Kennedy Library and Museum Home Page,* June 6, 1996, <http://www.cs.umb.edu/jfklibrary/j012061.htm> (May 23, 2003).

20 George Esper, *The Eyewitness History of the Vietnam War, 1961–1975* (New York: Villard Books, 1983), 3.

22 Ibid., 33.

24 "The President's Address," *New York Times,* August 5, 1964.

24 "Teacher's Guide, Echoes from the Wall, Appendix for Module One," *Teach Vietnam: The Learning Experience,* n.d., <http://www.teachvietnam.org> (May 23, 2003).

24 "Lyndon B. Johnson, 1908–1973," *Newsweek,* February 5, 1973, 31,34.

24 John Pimlott, *Vietnam: The Decisive Battles* (New York: MacMillan Publishing Company, 1990), 58.

25 U.S. Department of State, "Ambassador Taylor's Visit to Washington, September 6–10," *Foreign Relations of the United States, 1964–1968,* vol. 1, (Washington, D.C.: GPO, 1992).

25 Michael Beschloss, ed., *Reaching for Glory: Lyndon Johnson's Secret White House Tapes, 1963–1964* (New York: Simon & Schuster, 2001), 173–74.

26 PBS Online, "Transcript—LBJ Goes to War," *The American Experience: Vietnam Online,* 1997, <http://www.pbs.org/wgbh/amex/vietnam/104ts.html> (May 23, 2003).

26 Karnow, *Vietnam,* 432.

27 PBS Online, "Transcript—LBJ Goes to War," *The American Experience: Vietnam Online.*

27 "Transcript of the President's News Conference on Foreign and Domestic Affairs," *New York Times,* July 29, 1965.

30 Bernard Edelman, ed., *Dear America: Letters Home from Vietnam* (New York: Pocket Books, 1988), 113.

31 Ibid., 31–32.

35 Tang, *Viet Cong Memoir,* 157–158.

36 Gurney, *Vietnam: The War in the Air,* 109.

40 "William Westmoreland, Eagle Scout," *U.S. News and World Report,* March 16, 1998, 73.

40 PBS Online, "Transcript—The Tet Offensive," *The American Experience: Vietnam Online,* 1997, <http://www.pbs.org/wgbh/amex/vietnam/107ts.html> (May 23, 2003).

42 *Time,* February 16, 1968, 38.

42 CNN Interactive, "Episode Script," *The Cold War: Episode 11, Vietnam,* n.d., <http://www.cnn.com/SPECIALS/cold.war/episodes/11/script.html> (May 23, 2003).

44 Tobias Wolff, *In Pharaoh's Army: Memories of the Lost War* (New York: Alfred A. Knopf, 1994), 132.

45 Jonathan Schell, *The Real War: The Classic Reporting on the Vietnam War* (New York: Pantheon Books, 1987), 37.

45 The History Place, "The Vietnam War: The Jungle War, 1965–1968," *Historyplace.com,* n.d., <http://www.historyplace.com/unitedstates/vietnam/index-1965.html> (May 23, 2003).

45 Wallace Terry, *Bloods: An Oral History of the Vietnam War by Black Veterans* (New York: Random House, 1984), 23.

46 Austin Bunn, "Unarmed and under Fire: An Oral History of Female Vietnam Vets," *Salon.com,* November 11, 1999,

<http://archive.salon.com/mwt/feature/1999/11/11/women/index.html> (May 23, 2003).

46 Dan Freedman, ed., *Nurses in Vietnam* (Austin: Texas Monthly Press, 1987), 12.

47 Terry, *Bloods,* 62.

47 Ibid., 245.

48 C. L. Sulzberger, "A Tree Grows in Texas," *New York Times,* January 24, 1973. Reprinted on the Web at <http://www.nytimes.com/books/98/04/12/specials/johnson–tree.html> (May 23, 2003).

48 "Teacher's Guide, Echoes from the Wall, Appendix for Module Three," *Teach Vietnam: The Learning Experience,* n.d., <http://www.teachvietnam.org> (May 23, 2003).

49 Lyndon Baines Johnson, "The President's Address to the Nation Announcing Steps to Limit the War in Vietnam and Reporting His Decision Not to Seek Reelection, March 31, 1968," *Lyndon Baines Johnson Library and Museum Home Page,* February 18, 2002, <http://www.lbjlib.utexas.edu/johnson/archives.hom/speeches.hom/680331.asp> (May 23, 2003).

49 Ibid.

50 "Richard Milhous Nixon," *Central Washington University Home Page,* n.d., <http://www.cwu.edu/~millerj/writings/nixon.html> (May 23, 2003).

51 Janet Gilmore, "Fresh Behind–the–Scenes Look at Free Speech Movement," *University of California–Berkeley Home Page,* August 12, 2002, <http://www.berkeley.edu/news/media/releases/2002/08/12_book.html> (May 23, 2003).

51 PBS Online, "Transcript—LBJ Goes to War," *The American Experience: Vietnam Online.*

52 Esper, *Eyewitness History,* 122.

53 Harry G. Summers Jr., "Hamburger Hill Revisited," *Vietnam Magazine,* June 1999.

53 Charlie Cargo, "Wolf and Charlie," *Scout Dog Pages,* n.d., <http://www.scoutdogpages.com/wolfcharlie.htm> (May 23, 2003).

53 Tom L. Farley, "9th Division Scout Dogs," *Vietnam Dog Handler Association Home Page*, n.d., <http://www.vdhaonline.org/Dogman/arch_9th2.asp> (May 23, 2003).

54 Freedman, *Nurses in Vietnam,* 61.

55 Ibid., 62.

55 Ibid., 29.

56 Edelman, *Dear America,* 18.

56 Esper, *Eyewitness History,* 133.

56 The History Place, "The Vietnam War: The Bitter End, 1969–1975," *Historyplace.com,* n.d., <http://www.historyplace.com/unitedstates/vietnam/index-1969.html> (May 23, 2003).

57 Freedman, *Nurses in Vietnam,* 83.

57 "Text of President Nixon's Address to Nation on U.S. Policy in the War in Vietnam," *New York Times,* November 4, 1969.

58 "Transcript of President's Address to the Nation on Military Action in Cambodia," *New York Times,* May 1, 1970.

60 Esper, *Eyewitness History,* 151.

61 Doan Van Toai, "A Lament for Vietnam," *New York Times Magazine,* March 29, 1981. Reprinted on the Web at <http://www.nytimes.com/library/world/asia/032981vietnam-mag.html> (May 23, 2003).

62 "Transcript of Kissinger's News Conference on the Status of the Cease-Fire Talks," *New York Times,* October 27, 1972.

64 "The Paris Peace Accords," *Vietnam Magazine,* April 2000.

64 PBS Online, "Reflections," *The American Experience: Vietnam Online,* 1997, <http://www.pbs.org/wgbh/vietnam/reflect/hackworth.html> (May 23, 2003).

64 Harry G. Summers Jr., "The Bitter End," *Vietnam Magazine,* April 1995.

67 Malcom W. Browne, "Saigon's Finale," *New York Times Learning Network,* October 13, 1999, <http://www.nytimes.com/learning/general/specials/saigon/introduction_full.html> (May 23, 2003).

67 Malcolm W. Browne, "Thieu Resigns, Calls U.S. Untrustworthy," *New York Times,* April 22, 1975.

69 Tang, *Viet Cong Memoir,* 268.

69 Toai, "A Lament for Vietnam."

72 Brent Ashabranner, *Always to Remember: The Story of the Vietnam Veterans Memorial* (New York: Dodd, Mead & Company, 1988), 29.

SELECTED BIBLIOGRAPHY

Belshaw, Jim. "Tough Love: Doris 'Lucki' Allen in Vietnam." *The Veteran Magazine,* February/March 1999. Reprinted on the Web at <http://www.vva.org/TheVeteran/1999_03/lucki.htm> (May 28, 2003).

Beschloss, Michael, ed. *Reaching for Glory: Lyndon Johnson's Secret White House Tapes, 1964–1965.* New York: Simon & Schuster, 2001.

Bonds, Ray, ed. *The Vietnam War: The Illustrated History of the Conflict in Southeast Asia.* New York: Crown Publishers, Inc., 1983.

Browne, Malcolm W. "Da Nang's Fall Feared Imminent; U.S. Ships Sent to Help Refugees." *New York Times,* March 30, 1975. Reprinted on the Web at <http://www.nytimes.com/learning/general/specials/saigon/danang.html> (May 28, 2003).

____. "Saigon's Finale." *New York Times Learning Network,* October 13, 1999. Reprinted on the Web at <http://www.nytimes.com/learning/general/specials/saigon/introduction_full.html> (May 28, 2003).

Bunn, Austin. "Unarmed and under Fire: An Oral History of Female Vietnam Vets," *Salon.com,* November 11, 1999. <http://archive.salon.com/mwt/feature/1999/11/11/women/index.html> (May 28, 2003).

Butterfield, Fox. "Panic Rises in Saigon, but the Exits Are Few." *New York Times,* April 24, 1975. Reprinted on the Web at <http://www.nytimes.com/learning/general/specials/saigon/butterfield-article1.html> (May 28, 2003).

Calbreath, Jim. "A Day in the Life of . . . 18th Surgical Hospital." *The Vietnam War Internet Project*, June 12, 2001. <http://www.vwip.org/articles/c/CalbreathJim_DayInTheLifeOF18thSurgicalHospital.htm> (May 28, 2003).

Caputo, Philip. *A Rumor of War.* New York: Holt, Rinehart and Winston, 1977.

Dannenberg, James. "What I Did Was Legal, but Was It Right?" *Newsweek,* February 18, 2002, 19.

"Demonstrations Revisited," *Online NewsHour,* April 28, 2000. Transcript of PBS program, reprinted on the Web at <http://www.pbs.org/newshour/bb/asia/vietnam/vietnam_4-28.html> (May 28, 2003).

Donovan, David. *Once a Warrior King: Memories of an Officer in Vietnam.* New York: McGraw-Hill, 1985.

Dorr, Robert F. *Air War—Hanoi.* London: Blandford Press, 1988.

"Echoes of My Lai," *Time International,* March 16, 1998, 22.

Edelman, Bernard, ed. *Dear America: Letters Home from Vietnam.* New York: Pocket Books, 1988.

Esper, George. *The Eyewitness History of the Vietnam War, 1961–1975.* New York: Villard Books, 1983.

Freedman, Dan, ed., *Nurses in Vietnam.* Austin: Texas Monthly Press, 1987.

Gelb, Leslie H. "Vietnam, Test of Presidents, Was Distant War and Battle at Home." *New York Times,* May 1, 1975. Reprinted on the Web at <http://www.nytimes.com/learning/general/specials/saigon/sixpresidents.html> (May 28, 2003).

Greenberg, Martin H., and Augustus Richard Norton, eds. *Touring Nam: The Vietnam War Reader.* New York: William Morrow and Company, 1985.

Gurney, Gene. *Vietnam: The War in the Air.* New York: Crown Publishers, 1985.

Hanson, Victor Davis. "The Meaning of Tet." *American Heritage,* May 2001.

Karnow, Stanley. *Vietnam: A History.* New York: Penguin Books, 1991.

King Jr., Dr. Martin Luther. "Declaration of Independence from the War in Vietnam." *Ramparts,* May 1967, 33–37.

Lind, Michael. *Vietnam: The Necessary War.* New York: Free Press, 1999.

McDougall, Walter A. "Who Were We in Vietnam?" *New York Times on the Web,* April 26, 2000. <http://www.nytimes.com/library/opinion/042600oped-vietnam.html> (May 28, 2003).

McNamara, Robert S. *In Retrospect: The Tragedy and Lessons of Vietnam.* New York: Times Books, 1995.

Mohr, Charles. "History and Hindsight: Lessons from Vietnam," *New York Times,* April 30, 1985. Reprinted on the Web at <http://www.nytimes.com/library/world/asia/043085vietnam-lookback.html> (May 28, 2003).

Perlez, Jane. "New U.S. Consulate Opens in Saigon," *New York Times,* September 8, 1999. Reprinted on the Web at <http://www.nytimes.com/learning/general/specials/saigon/090899vietnam-us-consulate.html> (May 28, 2003).

Pimlott, John. *Vietnam: The Decisive Battles.* New York: MacMillan Publishing Company, 1990.

"Report of the Senate Select Committee on POW/MIA Affairs," *United States Senate,* January 13, 1993. <http://www.vwip.org/powssc-i.html> (May 28, 2003).

Santoli, Al, ed. *Everything We Had: An Oral History of the Vietnam War by Thirty-three American Soldiers Who Fought It.* New York: Ballantine Books, 1981.

Schell, Jonathan. *The Real War: The Classic Reporting on the Vietnam War.* New York: Pantheon Books, 1987.

Sheehan, Neil, et al. *The Pentagon Papers.* New York: Bantam Books, Inc., 1971.

Summers Jr., Harry G. *Historical Atlas of the Vietnam War.* New York: Houghton Mifflin Company, 1995.

Truong Nhu Tang. *A Viet Cong Memoir: An Inside Account of the Vietnam War and Its Aftermath.* New York: Vintage Books, 1985.

Terry, Wallace. *Bloods: An Oral History of the Vietnam War by Black Veterans.* New York: Random House, 1984.

Doan Van Toai. "A Lament for Vietnam." *New York Times Magazine,* March 29, 1981. Reprinted on the Web at <http://www.nytimes.com/library/world/asia/032981vietnam-mag.html> (May 28, 2003).

Tolan, Sandy. "The War Against the War." *American RadioWorks,* 2002. <http://www.americanradioworks.org/features/vietnam/us/waragainstwar.html> (May 28, 2003).

Tollefson, James W. *The Strength Not to Fight: An Oral History of Conscientious Objectors of the Vietnam War.* Boston: Little, Brown and Company, 1993.

United States Army Center for Military History Online. "Named Campaigns—Vietnam." n.d. <http://www.army.mil/cmh-pg/reference/vncmp.htm> (May 28, 2003).

"Vietnam Conflict Continues," *Newsweek,* March 4, 2002, 16.

"The Vietnam War," *Historyplace.com.* n.d. <http://www.historyplace.com/unitedstates/vietnamindex.html> (May 28, 2003).

"William Westmoreland, Eagle Scout," *U.S. News and World Report,* March 16, 1998, 73.

Witmer, John I. "South Vietnam's Collapse Is Documented," *Vietnam Magazine,* April 2000.

Wolff, Tobias. *In Pharaoh's Army: Memories of the Lost War.* New York: Alfred A. Knopf, 1994.

FURTHER READING AND WEBSITES

FURTHER READING

Anderson, Christopher J. *Grunts: U.S. Infantry in Vietnam*. Philadelphia: Chelsea House Publishers, 2000.

Ashabranner, Brent. *Always to Remember: The Story of the Vietnam Veterans Memorial*. New York: Dodd, Mead & Company, 1988.

Barr, Roger. *The Vietnam War*. San Diego, CA: Lucent Books, 1991.

Cima, Ronald J., ed. *Vietnam: A Country Study*. Washington, D.C.: Federal Research Service, Library of Congress, 1989.

Denenberg, Barry. *Voices from Vietnam*. New York: Scholastic Inc., 1995.

Devaney, John. *The Vietnam War*. New York: Franklin Watts, 1992.

Dudley, William, and David Bender, eds. *The Vietnam War: Opposing Viewpoints*. San Diego: Greenhaven Press, 1990.

Faas, Horst, and Tim Page, eds. *Requiem: By the Photographers Who Died in Vietnam and Indochina*. New York: Random House, 1997.

Galt, Margot Fortunato. *Stop This War! American Protest of the Conflict in Vietnam*. Minneapolis: Lerner Publications Company, 2000.

Gay, Kathlyn, and Martin Gay. *The Vietnam War*. New York: Twenty-First Century Books, 1996.

Lawson, Don. *An Album of the Vietnam War*. New York: Franklin Watts, 1986.

Levy, Debbie. *Lyndon B. Johnson*. Minneapolis: Lerner Publications Company, 2003.

Mabie, Margot C. J. *Vietnam, There and Here*. New York: Holt, Rinehart and Winston, 1985.

Márquez, Herón. *Richard M. Nixon*. Minneapolis: Lerner Publications Company, 2003.

Nickelson, Harry. *Vietnam*. San Diego: Lucent Books, 1989.

Sherman, Josepha. *The Cold War*. Minneapolis: Lerner Publications Company, 2004.

Taus-Bolstad, Stacy. *Vietnam in Pictures*. Minneapolis: Lerner Publications Company, 2003.

Willoughby, Douglas. *The Vietnam War*. Chicago: Heinemann Library, 2001.

Yancey, Diane. *The Vietnam War: Life of an American Soldier*. San Diego: Lucent Books, 2001.

WEBSITES

The American Experience: Vietnam Online. This website is the online companion to the award-winning PBS American Experience miniseries about the Vietnam War, *Vietnam: A Television History*. <http://www.pbs.org/wgbh/amex/vietnam>

"Ask a Reporter: Fox Butterfield," *New York Times on the Web*. This website features a profile of Fox Butterfield, a reporter who covered the Vietnam War in the 1970s. Mr. Butterfield also answers questions from students about the war. <http://www.nytimes.com/learning/general/specials/saigon/reporter.html>

Battlefield Vietnam. This is the companion website to the PBS miniseries, *Battlefield Vietnam*. <http://www.pbs.org/battlefieldvietnam>

The Cold War: Vietnam. This website from <CNN.com> discusses Vietnam as part of the Cold War, the global conflict between Communism and capitalism in the second half of the 1900s. <http://www.cnn.com/SPECIALS/cold.war/episodes/11>

Embassy of the Socialist Republic of Vietnam in the United States of America. Learn more about the Socialist Republic of Vietnam by visiting the website of its embassy in the United States. <http://www.vietnamembassy-usa.org>

"The Fall of Saigon," *New York Times on the Web Learning Network*. This website provides an index to both war era and recent *New York Times* articles about the Vietnam War as well as other special features. <http://www.nytimes.com/learning/general/specials/saigon>

Vietnam Dog Handler Association. This website honors "America's four-footed soldiers." <http://www.vdhaonline.org>

Vietnam—Echoes from The Wall. This is an educational tool created to help students learn about the Vietnam War and its impact on American society. <http://www.teachvietnam.org>

Vietnam: Echoes of War. Special features in this <CNN.com> website about the Vietnam War include stories about Dien Bien Phu, the Boat People, and Vietnam in recent years. <http://www.cnn.com/SPECIALS/2000/vietnam>

INDEX

ABOUT THE AUTHOR

Debbie Levy's *The Vietnam War* is her seventh non-fiction book for children. Her earlier books include the biography *Lyndon B. Johnson*. Levy earned a bachelor's degree in government and foreign affairs from the University of Virginia, as well as a law degree and master's degree in world politics from the University of Michigan. She practiced law with a large Washington, D.C., law firm and worked as a newspaper editor. Levy enjoys paddling around in kayaks and canoes and fishing in the Chesapeake Bay region. She lives with her husband and their two sons in Maryland.

PHOTO ACKNOWLEDGMENTS

The images in this book are used with the permission of: © Hulton-Deutsch Collection/CORBIS, pp. 4–5, 10, 17; © Russell L. Ciochon, p. 6; © Bettmann/ CORBIS, pp. 9, 15, 16, 18 (bottom), 21, 22, 25, 26, 28 (both), 29 (top), 30, 31, 33, 36, 49, 50, 51, 54, 55, 57, 58, 61, 63, 64, 66, 67, 69, 79 (top), 79 (second from top), 79 (second from bottom); National Archives, pp. 11, 12, 14, 18 (top), 32, 35 (bottom), 41, 42, 46, 47, 60, 62, 65, 78 (top), 78 (bottom); Library of Congress, pp. 13, 27; United States Army Military History Institute, p. 23; © Hulton/Archive by Getty Images, pp. 24, 59, 73; © Nik Wheeler/ CORBIS, p. 29; Department of Defense, pp. 34 (top), 79 (bottom); © CORBIS, p. 34 (bottom); © Wally McNamee/CORBIS, p. 35 (top); AP/Wide World Photos, pp. 38, 52; United States Army, pp. 40, 78 (second from bottom); UPI Photo by Kyoichi Sawada, p. 44; Corporal Nick Meyers/United States Marine Corps, p. 53; Southdale Hennepin Area Library, p. 56; © Francoise de Mulder/CORBIS, p. 68; United Nations High Commissioner for Refugees, p. 70; © Steve Raymer/CORBIS, p. 72; Independent Picture Service, p. 78 (second from top);

Cover by © Bettmann/CORBIS.